Thank You!
Psalm 139

JESUS JUICE FOR HEALTH & FREEDOM

by Tenickia Ernestine Polk

Jesus Juice for Health & Freedom
Copyright © 2015 by Tenickia Polk
All rights reserved.

Published by TP Rewards
8647 Richmond Highway #659
Alexandria, VA 22309
www.tp-rewards.com

No part of this publication may be reproduced, stored in a retrieval system or transmitted in any way by any means, electronic, mechanical, photocopy, recording or otherwise without written permission of the publisher except as provided by USA copyright law.

Scripture quotations are taken from the Holy Bible, King James Version (KJV) by public domain.

International Standard Book Number: 9780986065989

Published in the United States of America

~ To Women ~

Contents

Preface/7

Introduction: Blessed and Highly Favored/19

1. Healing (Replace Trauma with Forgiveness) /25
2. God Loves Women (Replace Rejection with Love) /45
3. Daddy's Girl (Replace Bondage with Adoption) /61
4. Very Good (Replace Accusation with Goodness) /81
5. Pathways (Replace Uncleanness with Holiness) /97
6. Personal Connection (Replace Occultism with a Personal Relationship with God) /115
7. Healthy You! /143

Preface

Statistics show women are 70% more likely than men to experience depression during their lifetime…BUT GOD! This book reveals the biblical principles every woman needs to pull down the strongholds blocking your true destiny. Finally, you can take a look into the mirror and see yourself as the strong woman God designed. This book will help you get rid of the spirits that can make you feel rejected, unclean and unworthy. This book will help you overcome obstacles and trauma, move from victim to victor, and encourage yourself and others in the Lord.

Jesus is God's answer, the best answer, for our sickness and problems: spirit, soul and body. However, we don't always know how to put this knowledge into practice. "Jesus Juice for Healing and Deliverance" will help you with that. The Bible instructs us to be a "doer" of the Word. "But be ye doers of the word, and not hearers only, deceiving your own selves" (James 1:22).

I started writing this book during the most trying time of my life. I had just separated from my ex-husband, and was facing all that comes with legal battles, domestic abuse, homelessness, unemployment, another miscarriage, and unbelievable health issues. I was oh so sick and I had no idea where my next meal would come from day to day. God delivered me, though. And He helps me overcome my daily battles. I am a witness that God delivers as He promises!

During these hard times, God revealed to me how I'd been duped by the devil about my struggle and my identity in Christ. Satan's kingdom had been telling me that the only way I'd be happy is if I somehow "fixed" a few things about myself, and if I stayed clear of my ex-husband. It was a lie. God, through His Word, taught me that I wasn't fighting myself, or even my ex-husband…I was fighting Satan's kingdom, and God had already equipped me to win (Ephesians 6:12: "For we wrestle not against flesh and blood, but against principalities, against powers, against the rulers of the darkness of this world, against spiritual wickedness in high places"). The enemy had distorted my view to mask himself, my true enemy.

I was a dedicated Christian when my life fell apart. I was an award-winning teacher in my church's elementary school in

Washington, DC. I volunteered regularly with the homeless, and I was a pretty good wife by conventional standards. I did everything I knew to do to stay in right standing with God. This is why I was so taken aback when my life suddenly fell apart. I didn't see it coming, but God did and He had already orchestrated a masterplan to bring me to His loving arms, and show me who I really am in Him. The wonderful life I thought I created before my divorce is now slowly being replaced with God's perfect will for me. And it feels so good!

This book is largely based on my personal research and application, initiated by my ministry experience at Be in Health in Thomaston, GA. The lessons explore some of the evil spirits I've personally come to recognize, as well as the Bible-based weapons you can use to overcome them. Evil spirits aren't the spooky ghost type beings that show up in your closet at night. Rather, they can consist of the spirituality passed down to you from your parents and prior generations. They are spirits that took advantage of trauma you may have experienced. They are spirits that we sometimes brush off as bad emotions—evil spirits like fear, rejection, bitterness, self-pity, etc. They are very real, and they can affect the lives of believers and unbelievers alike. The good news is that God has given us authority over these evil spirits (Luke 10:19: "Behold, I give unto you power to tread on serpents and scorpions, and over all the power of the enemy: and nothing shall by any means hurt you"). Ladies, this book teaches you how to identify and get rid of these hindrances (and achieve deliverance) in Jesus' name. I hate the devil…let's kick some devil butt!

My Testimony

I must stop to acknowledge Archbishop Alfred Owens, Jr., my pastor at Greater Mount Calvary Holy Church in Washington, DC. It was Archbishop Owens's voice that helped to deliver me from my abusive marriage. I called him a few days following my separation, when I first learned I was miscarrying my baby. He listened carefully to what I had to say and then he gently asked me, "Why would you want to stay with someone who treats you like that?" I was amazed. Was this a pastor, a bishop even, telling me it was ok to separate from my husband, my abusive husband? For the first time I began to entertain the idea that God cared about my well-being regardless of the marriage. It may sound strange, but up until this point, I'd understood that I was supposed to love other people, but never did I consider loving myself beyond survival and superficial displays like clothes and spa treatments. I'd been duped by the devil!

The day I talked with Archbishop Owens, my ex-husband sent me a Facebook message with a photo of our wedding day. When I told Archbishop Owens this, his response was, "Don't you still have a protection order against him? He's not supposed to be contacting you!" He was right! My life, peace and sanity mattered. I reported the breach and that was the last communication I've had with him outside of court.

I don't know if ministers know how much influence they can have on people's lives. My family and friends gave me the same insight about my ex, but I didn't trust or believe them. At that time, I don't know if I would have trusted any voice other than my pastor's. When dealing with something so sacred to God, marriage, I wanted to make sure I was getting it right. And to me at that time, the voice closest to God's was Archbishop Owens's.

Oftentimes ministers are first responders in domestic violence issues and the like. Unfortunately, mine is the only positive interaction I'm aware of concerning domestic violence victims and their churches. Often, victims are brought in for couples counseling and told to pray and stay —both very bad practices. In fact, I received the same advice from ministers in my church before talking directly to Archbishop Owens. My experience with Archbishop Owens opened the doorway for God's love to enter and heal my heart.

When the bad times hit, I devoured the Bible in search of help and God's position concerning my problems. I remember telling God that I'd know He was going to deliver me if I experienced an earthquake, like the one that occurred before God delivered David in 2 Samuel 22. At the time, I said it flippantly, having never experienced an earthquake because I lived on the east coast, in northern Virginia.

Well, the very next day, guess what happened? The 5.8 earthquake of 2011—the largest earthquake to rock Virginia in over 100 years! I hesitantly share this with you because I don't want you asking God for the same sign. But this was such a turning point in my life that I cannot omit it from this book. We serve a mighty God, and that earthquake showed me just how vulnerable we human beings really are. Certainly a God that could shake the earth for me could get me out of all the mess I was in, and He did.

I was most concerned with my health at the time, because my body was reacting to almost everything I ate and drank. I couldn't even shower or drink water because my body would react negatively. They call this multiple chemical sensitivities/environmental illness (MCS/EI), but I didn't know it at the time. I didn't know because I no longer had health insurance, so was unable to get a proper diagnosis. Before I became unemployed/uninsured, I had accrued a few diagnoses, though—lupus discoid, irritable bowel syndrome (IBS), depression, to name a few.

But once my insurance was done, I resorted to online research, vitamins and supplements for healing help. I purchased hundreds and maybe even thousands of dollars' worth of vitamins and supplements trying to get better. Most of the "remedies" helped for a brief period, but left me in greater bondage to the vitamins. I was confused, because nothing I tried had a lasting effect, yet I found so many examples of healing in the Bible.

"Lord, what do I have to do?" I cried in my heart.

Then one day while attending a domestic violence peer support group with The Women's Group of Mt. Vernon, I was introduced to the spiritual root causes of disease (by my friend Minister Donna Frazier) as taught by a ministry in Thomaston, GA, "Be in Health." I visited their website and learned that self-hatred was a root cause to lupus. At first I was appalled and offended, thinking, "I don't hate myself!" But when I started monitoring my thoughts, I realized just how true it was! The thoughts I had towards myself weren't kind at all. "You're the reason the marriage failed," "You'll never have a meaningful relationship," and the like.

I repented to God for self-hatred and started resisting those thoughts from the spirit of self-hatred, and very quickly lupus was gone. I read *A More Excellent Way* by Dr. Henry Wright, and took the "For My Life Training" at Be in Health, and that began my journey to truly loving God and understanding spiritual warfare. God delivered me from lupus, MCS/EI, candida, IBS, depression and more.

God is still doing a great work in my life. Never before have I been so free! God is my best friend and I enjoy spending time with him. The old song is true, "Can't nobody do me like Jesus." I'm so much more content with who I am and where I am in life. Because of this, God saw fit to trust me with serving other victims of domestic abuse as a member of the Fairfax County Domestic Violence Prevention, Policy and Coordinating Council, as the Vice President of The Women's Group of Mt. Vernon, and as the host of the TV show *Community Chat*. I've founded an educational ministry to help break the cycle of domestic abuse at www.domsticviolence.tv.

I'm forgiving my past, and I'm slowly learning to establish healthy, Godly relationships with men. To God be the glory!

Introduction

Blessed and Highly Favored

Sister girl, did you know that the person described in the Bible as blessed and highly favored is a woman, the Virgin Mary (Luke 28:1)? In this instance, to be blessed means to be spoken highly of. God spoke highly of Mary, a woman! You don't need a title to be special. You just need to know you are blessed and highly favored by God.

In this section, we'll receive a fresh view of our Father God and His plans for us as His daughters. Psychologists and theologians agree that a child's identity, to some extent, comes from their parents, especially their father. This is why I am dedicating this section to reintroducing you to your heavenly Father. Acts 17:27-30 sums up our goal for this chapter, stating:

27 That they should seek the Lord, if haply they might feel after him, and find him, though he be not far from every one of us:
28 For in him we live, and move, and have our being; as certain also of your own poets have said, For we are also his offspring.
29 Forasmuch then as we are the offspring of God, we ought not to think that the Godhead is like unto gold, or silver, or stone, graven by art and man's device.
30 And the times of this ignorance God winked at; but now commandeth all men every where to repent

Read the scripture above (Acts 17:27-30) again. What does it mean to you?

_____

_____

I know that once you understand your Father, you'll understand what it means to be a daughter, blessed and highly favored by God. As Paul introduced the Athenians to their "UNKNOWN GOD," so I aim to reintroduce you to the Godhead mentioned above in Acts 17. The Greek word for Godhead is *theios*, meaning God the Father, God the Son (Jesus), and God the Holy Spirit. Some people call the Godhead the "trinity," but it is called the Godhead in scripture.

All three members of the Godhead (Father, Son and Holy Spirit) make up the one God. It's just like each human being. We all have a body, a soul and a spirit that have different functions, but work together on behalf of the same person to make up the total person. Such is the case with the Godhead. In the Old Testament, this is the concept of unity of the Hebrew word "echad" found in Deuteronomy 6:4-5.

This section's lessons will place a special emphasis on God, our Father. Prayerfully work through each lesson, allowing God to reveal Himself to you afresh.

The Godhead

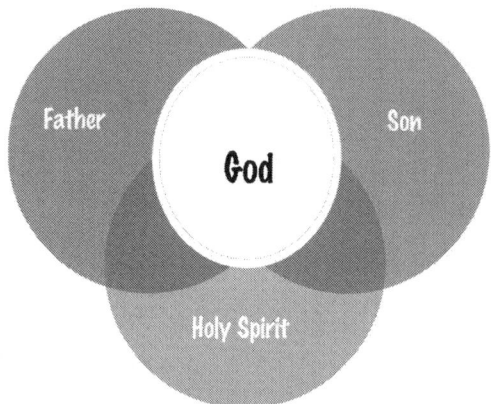

Human Being

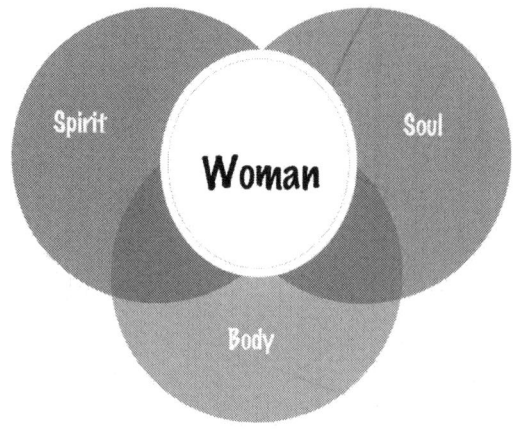

1
Healing
REPLACE TRAUMA WITH FORGIVENESS

1 Replace Trauma with Forgiveness

Have you experienced trauma? I cried enough tears for a lifetime during the summer of 2010. It was hard to believe that just three years prior, I had purchased my first house and was entering a marriage with the person I thought I would spend the rest of my life with—"till death do us part." What a shock to my soul to later realize that continuing the marriage could kill me: mind, body and soul. My marriage ended in 2010, and I also had to short-sale my home because we'd fallen so far behind in payments. After much prayer and counseling, I mustered up the courage to leave the abusive marriage.

I thought making the decision to leave would be the hardest part of my road to recovery, but I was wrong.

I had to obtain several protection orders from my ex-husband to successfully leave the relationship. This meant continuous court battles, first for protection orders, then eventually for a divorce. I had little money and so I depended heavily on nonprofits (The House of Ruth) and a childhood friend, Rasheed Allen Esq., to guide me through the legal process. And even with their help, I had to spend days on my own in the courthouse's law library.

On top of that, leaving the marriage left me homeless. As an educated single woman, I didn't think finding a place to stay would be as difficult as it turned out to be. I was still being paid as a teacher that summer, but my ex's refusal to contribute to household finances meant I had "bad credit." No one wanted to rent to me with bad credit and so I was homeless.

I moved among the homes of three different friends and family members before securing my own place that summer. This was tricky too. I couldn't live at some places because I feared my ex would find me, and I couldn't live with some people for fear of re-victimization. Domestic violence can happen among family and friends too…financially, emotionally, and mentally. I'd just gotten out of an abusive situation, and I really needed a place where I had peace. Thankfully, I came across a non-profit, Good Shepherd Housing, that helped me secure an apartment on my own.

Perhaps the most devastating event of summer 2010 was the diagnosis of another miscarriage—my third one! I could get over the failed marriage, but "Why oh why didn't God allow my baby to live?" I cried. "I am a woman, designed to bear children. What do I have to live for?" I wondered. "What will be my motivation to keep going?"

At the end of the summer, I decided it wasn't safe for me to return to my job as a school teacher because I didn't want to risk running into my ex. I didn't have a job for months, and this left me broke, with no health insurance. Daily meals were a matter of faith during this period.

As expected, my body didn't fare well throughout all this trauma. Because of various physical reactions, I could only safely eat one food—sweet potatoes. Thank God for sweet potatoes! I was so bound to food and chemical sensitivities. But God, through what I call Jesus Juice (the process of applying God's Word to my life), delivered me from these food sensitivities. He even healed me of some diseases like lupus and allergies that were diagnosed before I entered the abusive marriage.

In the summer of 2010, I'd experienced a boatload of trauma. I had nothing…but God.

Identifying Trauma

Chances are you've experienced trauma. Trauma is defined by Merriam Webster as "a very difficult or unpleasant experience that causes someone to have mental or emotional problems usually for a long time." The death of a loved one, accidents, illness, property loss, violence, threats of violence, sexual assault and rape, cults, domestic violence, witnessing violence, neglect, natural disasters, separation and even rejection can all be traumatic.

It is important to identify the traumatic experiences, because Satan, our enemy, often uses those experiences to open the door for evil spirits to enter our lives. When I say "evil spirits" I'm not referring to the ghosts you see in horror movies like *Nightmare on Elm Street*. An evil spirit can be anything that is contrary to the Word of God, like: **fear, bitterness, lust, unforgiveness, pride, envy, despair, violence, etc.** Experiencing a traumatic event can make us more susceptible to agreeing with evil spirits. We may think it's only "natural" to be fearful after being a victim of violence, but God says "God has not given you a spirit of fear: but of power, love and a sound mind" (2 Timothy 1:7). If it's not from God, it could be from an evil spirit (Ephesians 6:12: "For we wrestle not against flesh and blood, but against principalities, against powers, against the rulers of the darkness of this world, against spiritual wickedness in high places")...or it could be from you. But if it's not of God, it's not good (James: 1:17: "every good and perfect gift is from above, coming down from the Father of lights"), period. As believers, we aim to fill our lives with God's best (John 10:10: "The thief cometh not, but for to steal, and to kill, and to destroy: I am come that they might have life, and that they might have it more abundantly").

1. **Give an example of an evil spirit that may have entered your life through a traumatic event. For example, I was tempted with despair through my third miscarriage.**

_____

_____

Trauma in the Brain

Recently, I enjoyed an advocacy seminar on how the brain responds to trauma. The presenter described three parts of the brain: basal (reptilian), limbic (emotional) and neo-cortex (thinking). "Trauma," he said, "resides in the reptilian part of our brain; the lowest part that's similar to the makeup of a lizard or snake." He went on to explain that whenever a victim experiences a trigger (sights, sounds, smells, etc.) from their trauma, the reptilian brain is activated and the person can involuntarily go into panic, fear and other irrational behavior. I enjoyed the presentation, except for the fact that the data seemed to doom survivors to a life of fear. That's not the God I serve!

This reptilian brain sounded demonic to me (Revelation 20:2: "And he laid hold on the dragon, that old serpent, which is the devil, and Satan, and bound him a thousand years"), so I decided to see how it would stand against Jesus Juice. I raised my hand to let the facilitator know that in my work with survivors some have overcome their traumatic reactions by forgiving their abusers. To my surprise and delight, the presenter stopped, looked at me and explained that this is true: forgiveness takes place in the upper neo-cortex brain (the thinking brain); if a victim can activate the top of their head, it can override the activity in the reptilian brain.

Yes! I nearly hit the ceiling with joy—God's Word is true! This man, and science, had just confirmed God's Word. Carrying out God's Word (like forgiveness) activates our top brain, giving us power over that reptilian brain—the enemy (trauma). The following "Jesus Juice" lessons have been designed to help you recognize activities of the reptilian brain, and replace them with the godly principles that override them. Let's start by activating forgiveness. In my work with survivors, I've found that the only way to completely overcome trauma is by forgiving the abuser.

How to Forgive

How Forgiveness Works

There are two sides to forgiveness: (1) receiving forgiveness from God, and (2) forgiving others/yourself. So forgiveness is a double-sided coin; we give and receive it. "And when ye stand praying, forgive, if ye have ought against any: that your Father also which is in heaven may forgive you your trespasses. But if ye do not forgive, neither will your Father which is in heaven forgive your trespasses" (Mark 11:25-26).

Forgiveness is also a perfect equation concerning God: forgiving others = receiving forgiveness from God.

Repentance without forgiveness is void. We can see this in the example of the "unmerciful servant" in Matthew 18:23-35. The unmerciful servant asked for forgiveness, but refused to forgive his fellow servant. The master called the unmerciful servant "wicked" and threw him in jail.

Even though the unmerciful servant initially received forgiveness from his master, his forgiveness was revoked when the unmerciful servant wouldn't forgive his fellow servant. Jesus said, "So likewise shall my heavenly Father do also unto you, if ye from your hearts forgive not every one his brother their trespasses" (Matthew 18:35).

Greek definitions for key terms from *Strong's Concordance*

1. **Repent**: G3340, *metanoeo*—to think differently afterwards, i.e. reconsider (morally, feel compunction).
2. **Sin**: G266, *hamartia*—offence.
3. **Salvation**: G4991, *soteria*—rescue or safety (physically or morally):- deliver, health, salvation, save, saving.

4. **Forgiveness**: G859, *aphesis*—freedom; (figuratively) parson:- deliverance, forgiveness, liberty, remission.
5. **Forgive:** G863, *aphiemi* —forsake, lay aside, leave, let (alone, be, go, have), omit, put (send) away, remit, suffer, yield up.
6. **Forgive** [used in Luke 6:37 only]: G630, *apolyo*—to free fully, i.e (literally) relieve, release, dismiss, pardon or (specially) divorce.
7. **Faith:** G3982, *pistis*—persuasion, i.e. credence; moral conviction (of religious truth, or the truthfulness of God or a religious teacher), especially reliance upon Christ for salvation; abstractly, constancy in such profession; by extension, the system of religious (Gospel) truth itself:- assurance, belief, believe, faith, fidelity.

Receiving God's Forgiveness

In the Bible

Read Luke 7:37-50. The lady described as a "sinner" shows us how we can come to God for forgiveness of all of our sins.

Most sins (except blasphemy of the Holy Spirit) are recognized as forgivable by God in the Bible. We offend God with our sin, and thereby owe a debt to Him when we transgress His Word. 1 John 1:19 reminds us, "If we confess our sins, he is faithful and just and will forgive us our sins and purify us from all unrighteousness."

Here we find the sinful woman kissing Jesus' feet, washing Jesus' feet with her tears and hair, and anointing him with oil. Jesus explains that she loves Him more than the Pharisee because she'd been forgiven of more sin. This woman demonstrates how we should be exceedingly grateful in repentance. The more sin we recognize in our lives, the more we repent, the more grateful we are to God, and the more we serve and worship God.

2. Is there a limit to the number of sins God will forgive? Why or why not?

_____

_____

3. Is there a limit to the number of times God will forgive you? Why or why not?

_____

_____

4. Is being forgiven of your sins the same as receiving salvation through Jesus? Why or why not?

_____

_____

Forgiving Others

There are three categories we can consider when we forgive:
- God
- Self
- Others

Forgive God? What! How can we forgive God if He never does anything wrong? I agree that God is perfect. However, we (humanity), are not perfect and don't always understand

His ways. In light of the definition of forgive listed above (forsake, lay aside, leave, let alone), I believe we absolutely can and should forgive God.

The reason is because forgiveness is more about the person forgiving than the person who may have created the offense. **To forgive is an action of the person offended.** So we can practice forgiveness even if the person actually hasn't done anything wrong. For an example, a small child may learn to forgive their parent for a punishment they received for playing in the street. Is the child offended by the punishment? Yes! Did the parent actually do anything wrong to the child? No.

Getting back to forgiving God…women are sometimes "offended" by the way God created them to look, for being born into a certain family/race/class or even because of an untimely death of a loved one. Also, women can get upset with God for creating them female, instead of male.

While we know God's way of thinking surpasses ours (Isaiah 55:9: "For *as* the heavens are higher than the earth, so are my ways higher than your ways, and my thoughts than your thoughts."), we don't always agree with Gods ways. Be honest with God. Let Him know when you don't understand or agree with His ways. But ultimately we have to accept and forgive what God designs or allows. We can forgive God's righteous decisions. Often times I find that when I've forgiven God, He'll eventually give me satisfactory reasons for why things happened the way they did.

How to forgive:
Forgiving someone doesn't necessarily mean we have to talk to them or spend time with them. In fact, that could be a very naïve move and could cause us even more damage. Forgiveness takes place in our hearts. If it involves someone reasonable, yes, we can express our forgiveness to the other person. But, if we're forgiving an abuser…we can forgive them, but we don't have to reconcile with them. We don't have to tell an abuser, "I forgive you."

Sometimes we've been holding bitterness against people so often for so long we need deliverance from a spirit of unforgiveness. Other times, we just need to confess that we forgive a person with our mouths. Even if the other person isn't around, we can say aloud "I forgive xyz for xyz" every time we have a bitter thought towards them.

Praying for the people we forgive can also be helpful. I don't mean a simple "Lord bless them" prayer; I mean sincerely asking God to meet that person's needs for 2-5 minutes. "But I say unto you, Love your enemies, bless them that curse you, do good to them that hate you, and pray for them which despitefully use you, and persecute you" (Matthew 5:44).

Believe it in your heart (forgive in your heart) and confess it with your mouth. Say it aloud!

When to forgive:
We don't have to wait for a person to repent or apologize before forgiving them. Jesus asked Father God to forgive the crowd when he was dying on the cross, saying, "Father, forgive them; for they know not what they do" (Luke 23:34). Additionally, we should forgive:

- When we're upset about a situation
- When someone has wronged us
- When we've wronged others
- Daily, every second of the day, whenever there is a need

Missing the mark? What to do when forgiving is challenging:

Repent. Ask God for forgiveness for participating with a spirit of unforgiveness. The spirit of unforgiveness can be a strongman in our lives. At this point you may also need deliverance. You can cast the spirit of unforgiveness out of your life in the name of Jesus Christ of Nazareth (2 Timothy 2:26: "And *that* they may recover themselves out of the snare of the devil, who are taken captive by him at his will"). But be careful you're equipped to adequately resist the devil in the area of unforgiveness before casting it out; otherwise it can come back and give you much more trouble. "Then goeth he, and taketh with himself seven other spirits more wicked than himself, and they enter in and dwell there: and the last *state* of that man is worse than the first" (Matthew 12:45). We'll have to fight with praise and the truth of God's Word to stay free.

The Fight

We fight unforgiveness with God's Word. Recite the following FatherPa prayer model to combat unforgiveness. I developed this prayer model from the Lord's Prayer in Matthew 6:9-13. Say it aloud to be effective (Proverbs 18:21).

Forgiveness Ask God for forgiveness and forgive others	Father God, please forgive me for agreeing with the spirit of unforgiveness. I forgive myself for agreeing with the spirit of unforgiveness. Also, I forgive _____ for _____. I release them. He/she doesn't owe me anything. Thank you for forgiving me. [Take time to profess forgiveness of anyone you have a problem with, especially concerning rejection, but in other areas too. Consider whether you need to forgive God, yourself and/or others. The other person doesn't always have to be present. God forgives us as we forgive others (Mark 11:26)].
Avoid temptation	Help me not to be tested with unforgiveness beyond what I'm able to bear. Help me resist the devil. And when I'm tempted to agree with unforgiveness, show me the way out. Show me the way of escape you promised (1 Corinthians 10:13).
Truth	Father, you are forgiving.
His will	I receive your forgiveness.
Eternal praise	You are worthy to be praised. You are the one wise God.

Rescue me	Deliver me from the spirit of unforgiveness. I can't do it on my own. Please deliver me through the blood of Jesus.
Provision daily	Remind me daily I am to forgive others as you've forgiven me.
Agree with God	Thank you for delivering me from a spirit of unforgiveness. You forgive me. I receive your forgiveness. In the name of Jesus Christ of Nazareth I pray. Amen

2

God Loves Women
Replace Rejection with Love

2 Replace Rejection with Love

As a child, I remember a family member saying, "I wanted all of my children to be boys." I don't remember if they were talking to me, but those words stuck with me.

I probably shouldn't have been offended by those words, because I think they said it right after one of their sons had just gotten into some trouble, and they may have said it as if to say, "I don't wish I had all boys now, because this boy is too much!" That's my assumption though. They didn't finish their statement, and the statement left me feeling rejected through my adulthood. After all, I was a girl—even "a good girl." Why wouldn't they want me?

There are countless other women who share similar stories. Just this morning I read about President Obama's mother, Stanley Ann Dunham, who was named "Stanley" after her dad because he wanted a boy. She later went by "Ann" of course.

The fact that I still remember exactly where I was when I heard this family member say they wanted boys, although I can't remember what I wore last week, lets me know this was a doorpoint for the spirit of rejection to enter my life. Rejection can come from other doors like achievement, race, class, education, etc. But far too often, women can live their entire lives feeling rejected, just because they're a woman.

This lesson will teach you how to replace the spirit of rejection with God's love.

IDENTIFYING REJECTION

Ladies, we know that our battle to receive God's love is not against ourselves, or other people; our battle is against evil spirits (Ephesians 6:12). One of the primary evil spirits working to block God's love is the **spirit of rejection**.

Rejection is one of women's biggest obstacles to receiving God's love. Simply put, we agree with the spirit of rejection whenever we think "you don't love me," or "you don't like me." We can even entertain these thoughts against ourselves, thinking "I don't measure up."

Women around the world are rejected in homes, in churches, in the workplace, in government and even at birth. Some cultures reverence the birth of a boy child over the birth of a girl. But take heart, ladies: we're in good company! Our Lord and Savior Jesus Christ was also rejected (Isaiah 53:3: "He is despised and rejected of men; a man of sorrows, and acquainted with grief: and we hid as it were our faces from him; he was despised, and we esteemed him not"). But Jesus never agreed with the rejection of others. He always knew His power and identity as the Son of God. Likewise, we must remember our identity as daughters of God.

While others may reject us, we can never accuse God of rejecting us. God is love (1 John 4:8). If someone doesn't like you, that's their sin. However, it can become your sin too if you agree with their rejection of you. God may disapprove of our behavior, but never rejects us. God is always standing with open arms to receive his children (Romans 8:15: "For ye have not received the spirit of bondage again to fear; but ye have received the Spirit of adoption, whereby we cry, Abba, Father").

All we really need is God's *agape* love. He may use other people to demonstrate His love, but all love comes from Him (James 1:17: "Every good gift and every perfect gift is from above, and cometh down from the Father of lights").

> How does it make you feel to know Jesus was rejected?

The Fight

We fight rejection with God's Word. Recite the following FatherPa prayer model to combat rejection. I developed this prayer model from the Lord's Prayer in Matthew 6:9-13. It is helpful for deliverance and protection from a spirit of rejection.

Take a moment to repent (aloud) for any rejections you may have participated with. You can say **"Father God, I repent (change my mind) for participating with the rejection."**

Now, you can use the following FatherPa prayer model to profess a rejection deliverance prayer aloud. Say it aloud to be effective (Proverbs 18:21).

Forgiveness Ask God for forgiveness and forgive others	Father God, please forgive me for agreeing with the spirit of rejection. I forgive myself for agreeing with the spirit of rejection. Also, I forgive _____ for _____. Thank you for forgiving me. [Take time to profess forgiveness of anyone you have a problem with, especially concerning rejection, but in other areas too. Consider whether you need to forgive God, yourself and/or others. The other person doesn't always have to be present. God forgives us as we forgive others (Mark 11:26)].

REPLACE REJECTION WITH LOVE

Avoid temptation	Help me not to be tested with rejection beyond what I'm able to bear. Help me resist the devil. And when I'm tempted to agree with rejection, show me the way out. Show me the way of escape you promised (1 Corinthians 10:13).
Truth	Father, you are love.
His will	I receive your love.
Eternal praise	You are worthy to be praised. You are the one wise God.
Rescue me	Deliver me from the spirit of rejection. I can't do it on my own. Please deliver me through the blood of Jesus.
Provision daily	Remind me daily that I am the apple of your eye, that you are my defender and that you are my redeemer. Thank you for making me a woman.
Agree with God	Thank you for delivering me from a spirit of rejection. You love me. I receive your love. In the name of Jesus Christ of Nazareth I pray. Amen

God Loves Women

No matter your state in life, God loves you! "For God is love" (1 John 4:8). There is nothing you can do to make God love you more or less. "But God commendeth his love toward us, in that, while we were yet sinners, Christ died for us" (Romans 5:8).

In the Bible

Read John 8:3-11. We can see how much God loves women through this story of the woman caught in the act of adultery. In this story we see religious leaders pointing their finger at the woman, ready to kill her. We don't see anyone questioning the whereabouts of the man caught with the woman, only accusations and condemnation towards the woman. Then Jesus steps on the scene to the woman's defense. God is our defender! He saved the woman from death, even though she sinned. No, Jesus didn't condone her adulterous act, but he had mercy on her.

Sometimes women get treated unfairly, but God is right there with us, loving and defending us. God recognizes the sinful reality of our world, and He still decides to love us. His love supersedes the law, He Himself fulfilling the law for us on the cross. Instead of demanding the execution of the law, he showed the woman mercy and sent her on her way with a warning to "sin no more."

1. How was Jesus' reaction to the adulterous woman different from the reaction of the religious leaders?

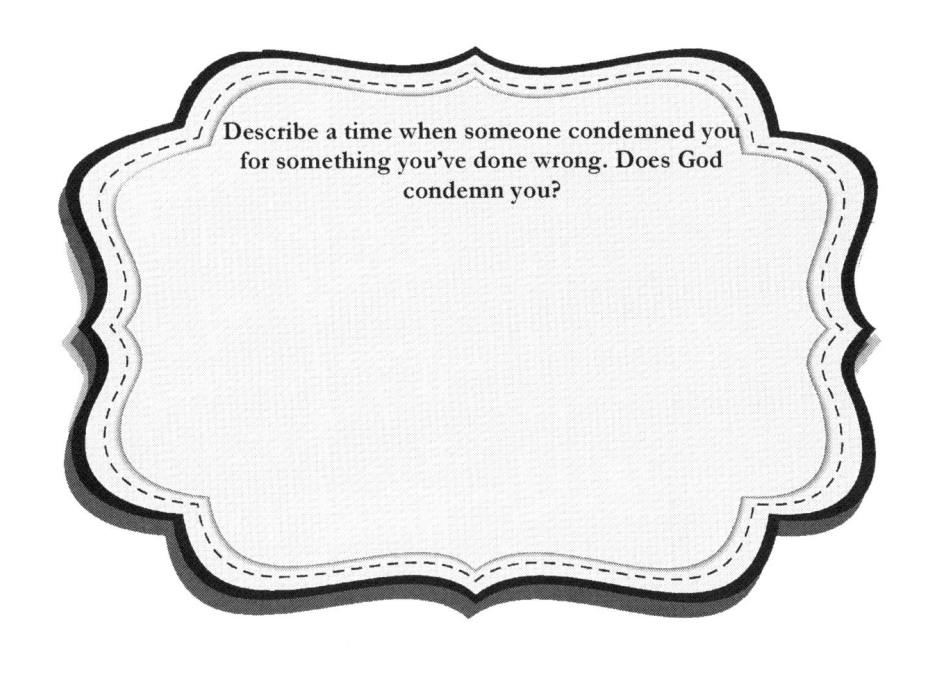

> Describe a time when someone condemned you for something you've done wrong. Does God condemn you?

What is love? There are several types of love mentioned in our Bible (King James Version), but the one used for God in 1 John 4:8 ("For God is love") is the Greek word *agape*. The Greek word *agape* is translated in our English Bible as "love" and sometimes it is translated as "charity." *Strong's Concordance* (G26) defines it as "**affection, good will, love, benevolence and brotherly love**." *Agape* love is also described in 1 Corinthians 13:4-8 as follows.

Greek meaning of love (Strong's Concordance #G26)- affection, good will, love, benevolence and brotherly love

1 Corinthians 13: 4-8
4 Charity suffereth long, and is kind; charity envieth not; charity vaunteth not itself, is not puffed up, 5 Doth not behave itself unseemly, seeketh not her own, is not easily provoked, thinketh no evil; 6 Rejoiceth not in iniquity, but rejoiceth in the truth; 7 Beareth all things, believeth all things, hopeth all things, endureth all things.
8 Charity never faileth: but whether there be prophecies, they shall fail; whether there be tongues, they shall cease; whether there be knowledge, it shall vanish away.

2. **What two characteristics of love stand out to you from the Greek definition or the definition in 1 Corinthians 13:4-8?**

---

3. **Which two characteristics of God's love are you most grateful to have in your life? Why?**

---

4. List 10 descriptions of agape love from the Greek definition and 1 Corinthians 13:4-8.

Putting It into Practice

God's love is unconditional; however, the enemy is always at work manufacturing thoughts, emotions and situations to make us believe just the opposite. He wants to destroy our relationship with God, by making us believe that God doesn't love us, that we're no good, and that God is accusing us…even as believers. The truth is:

1. **God is my redeemer.** Isaiah 47:4: "As for our redeemer, the Lord of hosts is his name, the Holy One of Israel."
2. **God is my defender.** Psalm 59:9-10: "Because of his strength will I wait upon thee: for God is my defence. The God of my mercy shall prevent me: God shall let me see my desire upon mine enemies."
3. **I am the apple of God's eye.** Zechariah 2:8: "For thus saith the Lord of hosts; After the glory hath he sent me unto the nations which spoiled you: for he that toucheth you toucheth the apple of his eye."

Know these truths, and when the devil brings you thoughts, emotions or situations that are just the opposite, we can resist him (James 4:7: "Submit yourselves therefore to God. Resist the devil, and he will flee from you") **by confessing these truths with our mouths. You are a daughter!**

Use the three aforementioned professions of truth to fill in the blanks below.

5. When I'm feeling worthless, I'll say

___

6. When it seems no one cares about me or my situation, I'll say

___

7. When I've messed up, I'll say

___

3
Daddy's Girl
Replace Bondage with Adoption

3 Replace Bondage with Adoption

I was a sexual slave to my ex-husband. We had sex just about every night, and not because I always wanted to. But if I didn't, he'd keep me up half of the night with emotional drama.

One night, I fell asleep without initiating sex (oh yeah, he preferred I initiated it), and he got so upset that he flipped the bed over while I was sleeping on it! I got off the floor, repositioned the mattress on the bed, and thanked God my ex-husband went to the guest room to sleep. "Hopefully he won't come back into the room tonight," I thought.

Most of the time I'd give in though. I feared that if I didn't, he'd go elsewhere for sexual gratification. I thought I was honoring God by complying with his requests, and would considered a "bad" Christian wife if I didn't. I worked to maintain the marriage without regard for my own well-being.

I was bound, thinking my ex-husband was the source of my love. I didn't understand Father God's unconditional love for me. This lesson will show you how to replace the spirit of bondage with God's unfailing love of adoption.

IDENTIFYING BONDAGE

Romans 8:15 explains, "For ye have not received the spirit of bondage again to fear; but ye have received the Spirit of adoption, whereby we cry, Abba, Father." However, the spirit of bondage says, "I have something better than what God is offering." It accuses God to us, saying, "You really won't get rewarded for obeying God." There are three main components of understanding the spirit of bondage. Understanding these components help us overcome bondage. The three elements of the spirit of bondage are:

1- it competes with God's promises and rewards;
2- it slanders God's name and loving character; and
3- it entraps us through fear of death and destruction.

Promises:

The spirit of bondage is an enslaving spirit that **competes with God's promises and rewards.** When we agree with a spirit of bondage, instead of adoption, our inheritance as daughters of God is clouded. Through Christ, Father God adopted believers into His family. Our inheritance as His daughters includes all the goodness God promises us here on earth, and his promises through salvation in heaven (our eternal prize).

Some of God's promises include:
- "For I know the thoughts that I think toward you, saith the Lord, thoughts of peace, and not of evil, to give you an expected end" (Jeremiah 29:11)
- "Come unto me, all ye that labour and are heavy laden, and I will give you rest. Take my yoke upon you, and learn of me; for I am meek and lowly in heart: and ye shall find rest unto your souls" (Matthew 11:28-29)
- "He giveth power to the faint; and to them that have no might he increaseth strength. Even the youths shall faint and be weary, and the young men shall utterly fall. But they that wait upon the Lord shall renew their strength; they shall mount up with wings as eagles; they

shall run, and not be weary; and they shall walk, and not faint" (Isaiah 40:29-31)
- "But my God shall supply all your need according to his riches in glory by Christ Jesus" (Phillipians 4:19)
- "For God so loved the world, that he gave his only begotten Son, that whosoever believeth in him should not perish, but have everlasting life" (John 3:16)

There are more like this. The spirit of bondage temps us by telling us these promises aren't true. Bondage says its promises of pleasure, wealth, power, fame etcetera are better than God's promises. Bondage is especially tempting to pleasure seekers.

Character:

The spirit of bondage **slanders God's name and loving character. It accuses God of being mean and withholding pleasure.** It lies to you and **tells you God doesn't really love you**; and that God will abandon you if you mess up. Making us feel like slaves on a plantation, the spirit of bondage paints a horrible image of Father God as a "meanie" in the sky, ready to beat us when we do something wrong. This is the wrong perception of God. Father God loves us and has adopted us into the family for His pleasure (Colossians 1:16).

He decided to take us in from the fields (Romans 8:15), provide for all our needs (Philippians 4:19) and nurture a father-daughter relationship with us (Revelation 3:20). The devil (bondage) is a liar. God is good!

Motivation:
The spirit of bondage **entraps us through fear of death and destruction** (Hebrews 2:15). This can be the fear of physical death or the loss of something so dear to you life may seem pointless without it. However, Paul explains how believers should view death in Philippians 1:21, saying, "for to me to live is Christ, and to die is gain."

Fear was one of the biggest reasons I stayed in an abusive marriage. Because I didn't know God, I feared disappointing Him if I separated. I also feared being lonely. This fear kept me in bondage. The spirit of bondage is a lying spirit because God promises to raise his children and give us eternal life (John 3:16: "For God so loved the world, that he gave his only begotten Son, that whosoever believeth in him should not perish, but have everlasting life"). Hold tight to God's truth and His loving heart towards us, ladies! God has not given us the spirit of fear, but of power, and of love, and of a sound mind (2 Timothy 1:7).

Addictions

We can most easily see bondage's work through **addictions**. Bondage uses almost anything, even something good from God, to enslave. I'll follow Paul's example here by being transparent about a personal battle (Romans 7:15: "For that which I do I allow not: for what I would, that do I not; but what I hate, that do I"). I battle a sleeping addiction. I can sometimes be found sleeping when God is telling me to do something else. I've noticed all three elements of bondage in this addiction as follows. (1) At the time, I bought the lie that the reward of my sleep is better than the reward of the task God is asking me to do (twisted reward). I hesitated to obey God, when I didn't understand why I had to do the certain task God asked me to do. Also, (2) I was fearful God wouldn't ever let me sleep (I know this is extreme!), when deep down inside (3) I questioned whether He really had my best interest in mind (questioning God's character). Lastly, sleep is comforting to me (pleasure seeker)—being wrapped up in my pillows and blanket. I turn to sleep to comfort myself, when I fear neither God nor anyone else will provide the comfort I want, even though He is the God of all comfort (2 Corinthians 1:3).

Certainly, I could have been more successful in business, and my living space would have been tidier if I didn't indulge in sleep. Also, often during my addictive sleep episodes, I'd experience nightmares. This same addiction pattern can be true for other addictions like drugs, alcohol, sex, food, exercise, gambling, etc. All these addictions are often used to sooth the pain of bondage and to avoid confronting problems.

Judgment and My Journey to Victory!

Once I finally recognized the addiction for what it was, I repented and cast out the spirit of sleep addiction in the name of Jesus Christ of Nazareth! But this deliverance prayer, however, didn't produce the victorious results I usually experience in other areas of my life.

So, I went back into my prayer closet and asked God why I was still struggling with this sleep addiction when I sincerely wanted to stop. The answer He revealed was simple, yet shocking. He showed me that I remained in bondage to sleep, because I was still holding a friend in bondage (through judgment) for her sleep addiction. God couldn't honor my prayer of repentance until I released my friend. I had to repent for judging my friend. "Therefore thou art inexcusable, O man, whosoever thou art that judgest: for **wherein thou judgest another, thou condemnest thyself; for thou that judgest doest the same things**" (Romans 2:1).

You see, I witnessed this friend sleep most of the time I've known her, from my youth till now. While I'd dare not say anything to her directly, I judged her as "lazy" in my heart. I was convicted to repentance for unforgiveness and judgmentalism towards my friend's sleeping habits. The scriptures are very clear on this subject:

Matthew 16:19
"And I will give unto thee the keys of the kingdom of heaven: and whatsoever thou shalt bind on earth shall be bound in heaven: and whatsoever thou shalt loose on earth shall be loosed in heaven."

1 John 1:9

"If we confess our sins, he is faithful and just and will forgive us our sins and purify us from all unrighteousness."

Matthew 7:1-3

"Judge not, that ye be not judged. For with what judgment ye judge, ye shall be judged: and with what measure ye mete, it shall be measured to you again."

I obtained a certain level of victory over the sleep addiction only when I repented for judging my friend for hers. Unfortunately, I've had to face this battle and repent more than once. Even today, whenever I find this friend sleeping my heart automatically wants to judge her…binding me to the same sin again. I am freed only when I remember to repent aloud and receive my forgiveness from God. Forgiveness can be an ongoing continuous process (Matthew 18: 21-22: "Then came Peter to him, and said, Lord, how oft shall my brother sin against me, and I forgive him? till seven times? Jesus saith unto him, I say not unto thee, Until seven times: but, Until seventy times seven").

More on victory…

The Merriam Webster definition of victory is to "overcome an enemy or antagonist." The common imagery we hold of obtaining a war victory still applies in the spirit realm. However, our roles and the rules change in spiritual warfare. Our enemy is Satan and his kingdom (Ephesians 6:12-13: "For we wrestle not against flesh and blood, but against principalities, against powers, against the rulers of the darkness of this world, against spiritual wickedness in high places. Wherefore take unto you the whole armour of God, that ye may be able to withstand in the evil day, and having done all, to stand."). Instead of fighting the enemy head-on with our own wisdom and strength; we obtain victory over the enemy when we submit to God's plan. God's ways are contrary to the natural instincts of our reptilian brain. For an example:

~Our reptilian brain says take, but God says give;
~Our reptilian brain says punish, but God says forgive; and
~Our reptilian brain says doubt, but God says trust.

When we follow God' plan, our good Shepherd fights for us (John 10:11: "I am the good shepherd: the good shepherd giveth his life for the sheep."). We are mere sheep being led by God to victory. (Psalm 23: "The Lord is my shepherd; I shall not want. He maketh me to lie down in green pastures: he leadeth me beside the still waters. He restoreth my soul: he leadeth me in the paths of righteousness for his name's sake. Yea, though I walk through the valley of the shadow of death, I will fear no evil: for thou art with me; thy rod and thy staff they comfort me. Thou preparest a table before me in the presence of mine enemies: thou anointest my head with oil; my cup runneth over. Surely goodness and mercy shall follow me all the days of my life: and I will dwell in the house of the Lord for ever.").

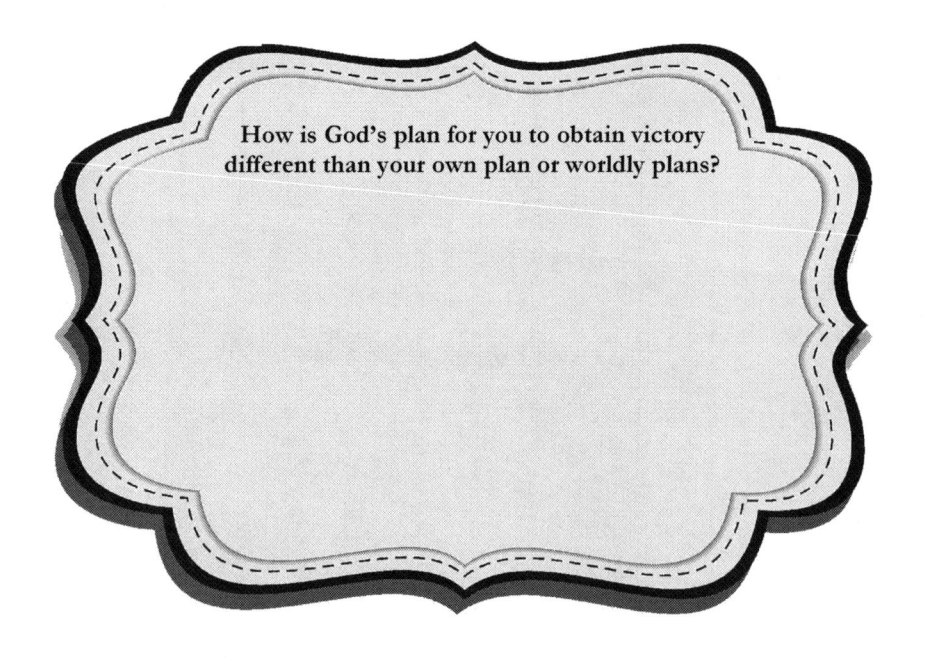

> **How is God's plan for you to obtain victory different than your own plan or worldly plans?**

The Fight

Take a moment to repent (aloud) for any addictions you may have participated with. You can say **"Father God, I repent (change my mind) for participating with the following addictions: _____, _____, _____, _____."**

Now, you can use the following FatherPa prayer model to confess a bondage deliverance prayer aloud.

Forgiveness — Ask God for forgiveness and forgive others	Father God, please forgive me for agreeing with the spirit of bondage by _____[insert addiction]_____. I forgive myself for agreeing with the spirit of bondage by _____[insert addiction]_____. Also, I forgive _____ for _____. Thank you for forgiving me. [Take time to profess forgiveness of anyone you have a problem with, especially concerning their participation with the spirit of bondage, but in other areas too. Consider whether you need to forgive God, yourself and/or others. The other person doesn't always have to be present. God forgives us as we forgive others (Mark 11:26)].
Avoid temptation	Help me not to be tested with the spirit of bondage by _____[insert addiction]_____ beyond what I'm able to bear. Help me resist the devil. And when I'm tempted to agree with bondage, show me the way out. Show me the way of escape you promised (1 Corinthians 10:13).

Truth	Father, thank you for setting me free.
His will	I receive your freedom.
Eternal praise	You are worthy to be praised. You are the one wise God.
Rescue me	Deliver me from the spirit of bondage by _____[insert addiction]_____. I can't do it on my own. Please deliver me through the blood of Jesus.
Provision daily	Remind me daily that you love me, that you are my Father and you've adopted me as your daughter, and that your promises are true.
Agree with God	Thank you for delivering me from a spirit of bondage by _____[insert addiction]_____. You love me. I receive your love. In the name of Jesus Christ of Nazareth I pray. Amen

DADDY'S GIRL

God is our true Father, and believers bear His identity. Our biological parents sometimes fall short in their parental responsibilities. What are we to do? We forgive them and know "though thy father and mother forsake me, the LORD will take me up" (Psalm 27:10). As we age, relationships with biological parents do and should change. However, our relationship with Father God remains the same (Ephesians 4:6: "One God and Father of all, who is above all, and through all, and in you all"). God will never forget us (Isaiah 49:15: "Can a woman forget her sucking child, that she should not have compassion on the son of her womb? yea, they may forget, yet will I not forget thee"). You are not a bastard or an orphan; you are not unwanted, you are not a mistake (Ephesians 1:5: "Having predestinated us unto the adoption of children by Jesus Christ to himself, according to the good pleasure of his will"). God created you for His delight (Col. 1:16: "For by him were all things created, that are in heaven, and that are in earth, visible and invisible, whether they be thrones, or dominions, or principalities, or powers: all things were created by him, and for him").

Being adopted by God means being obedient to Him and being a servant to righteousness (Romans 6:18: "Being then made free from sin, ye became the servants of righteousness"). We exchange our servitude to sin for a servitude to righteousness. Daughters of God are dead to the law of sin by the body of Christ. Instead, daughters of God follow the law of the Spirit. We are free from the law of sin

and death. (Romans 8:2: "For the law of the Spirit of life in Christ Jesus hath made me free from the law of sin and death").

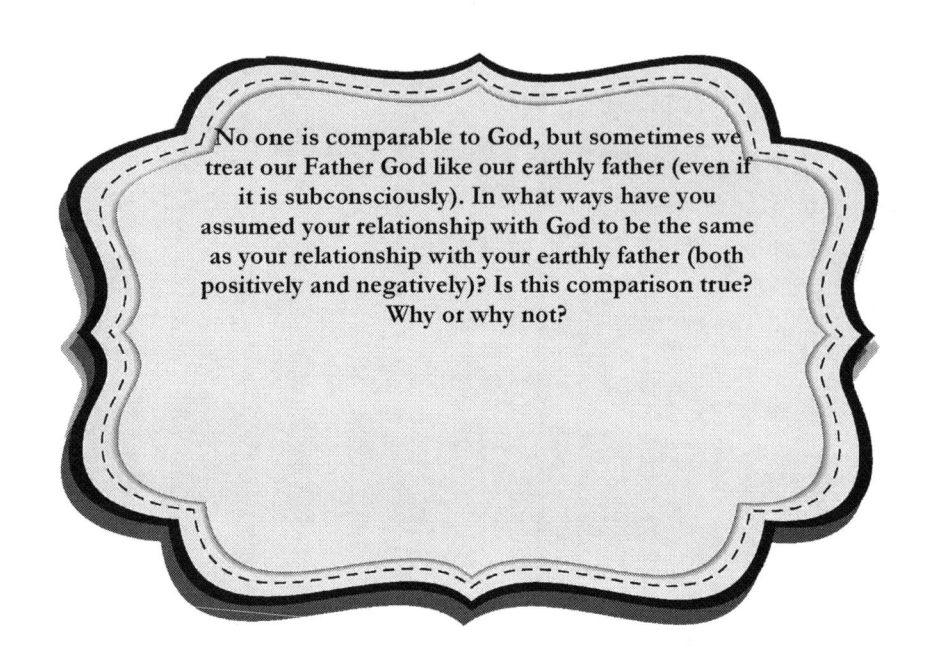

> No one is comparable to God, but sometimes we treat our Father God like our earthly father (even if it is subconsciously). In what ways have you assumed your relationship with God to be the same as your relationship with your earthly father (both positively and negatively)? Is this comparison true? Why or why not?

In the Bible

Read the book of Ester 2:7-8, 4:15-17, and 7:3-8:8. Ester was an orphan, both her parents were deceased, but God had a plan for her. Mordeci, her uncle, brought her up and advised Ester from childhood, but by the end of the book it is clear that Ester developed her own personal relationship with God, our Father. For when she and her people were in danger, she fasted and prayed to her Father, God, who delivered her and the Jews. Despite Ester's unfortunate beginnings, God raised her up to the palace and used her to deliver her people! God had a special plan for Ester and he has a special plan for you. Your family circumstances cannot hold back the hand of God in your life. A "father to the fatherless and a judge of the widows, is God in his holy habitation" (Psalm 68:5).

God should be recognized as the ultimate father of every woman, for it is God who has the power to deliver, save and heal. God is our loving father, daddy and papa.

1. Has God become your ultimate Father? Why or why not?

_____

_____

2. Do you turn to God first to meet your needs? Why or why not?

_____

_____

The Greek word for father is *pater* (G3962). It means a generator or male ancestor. The English dictionary definition of a generator is something that causes something else to arise or come about; a producer. As a metaphor, sometimes the word is used in the Bible to mean an originator and transmitter of anything. Father God is called the father of Jesus Christ (John 14:28: "I go unto the Father: for my Father is greater than I"). He is the Father, generator, of all spirits (Hebrews 12:9: "Furthermore we have had fathers of our flesh which corrected us, and we gave them reverence: shall we not much more readily be in subjection to the Father of spirits and live?"). He is our Father (Matthew 6:9: "After this manner therefore pray ye: Our Father which art in heaven, Hallowed be thy name").

Here's what we know about Father God:
- Everything good comes from our Father (James 1:17)
- He sits on a throne in heaven (Daniel 7:9)
- He is in heaven (Matthew 10:32)
- He has hair like pure wool (Daniel 7:9)
- He praised and honored Jesus (John 8:53)
- We pray to Him (Matthew 6:6)
- He sees all (Matthew 6:6)
- He forgives (Matthew 6:14)
- He knows all (Matthew 6:32, Luke 12:30)
- He is glorious (Mar 8:38)
- He is merciful (Luke 6:36)
- He is Lord of heaven and earth (Luke 10:21)
- He has a will
- He doesn't judge (John 5:22)
- There is only one Father (John 8:41)

- He hears us (John 11:41)

3. Which two of the characteristics surprised you about God, our Father? Why?

_____

_____

4. Give an example of a time when you've experienced God as your Father.

_____

_____

4
Very Good
Replace Accusation with Goodness

4 Replace Accusation with Goodness

I was raised in the T-Dog, a housing projects in Erie, PA. There, I was taught to always watch my back. I even had to be cautious not to fall into the schemes of certain family members. It was an art in our neighborhood, to see how much you can "get over" (take advantage of/victimize) someone…anyone. Family and friends often sat around laughing at the stupidity of their latest victim. This was very common.

I learned to see everyone in terms of extremes—a person was either good or bad, period. I tried to avoid the "bad" people, and I "got over" on the "good" people—that was the name of the game; that was life in the projects. I got what I could, when I could and never got too attached to anyone; not even family.

By God's grace I made it out of the projects, but I'm still learning how to develop healthy relationships. Like life in the projects, I still find myself looking for a reason to accuse someone of something, so I know whether they are safe. My relationship with God is no different and I'm still learning to fully trust Him. I do well in corporate America, because many professionals play with the same projects mentality to some extent. The only difference is that the people in corporate America have money, so their scheming and manipulation aren't as obvious.

I'm still extremely surprised when people genuinely do nice things for me. I'm better at doing nice things for others, though. Giving love can be difficult when we participate with accusation. Receiving love from others can be challenging when we participate with self-accusation.

This isn't how the Kingdom of God Works, though. Accusation is a spirit from Satan's kingdom. God is good and he created mankind as very good. Healthy relationships require us to replace accusations with goodness.

IDENTIFYING ACCUSATION

The *New Oxford American Dictionary*'s definition of accusation is "to charge or claim that someone has done something illegal or wrong." I imagine Satan as a prosecuting attorney standing before Judge God, telling Him why we deserve to die. Satan is our enemy (1 Peter 5:8: "Your adversary the devil, as a roaring lion, walketh about, seeking whom he may devour") and accusation is perhaps the most devastating spirit he uses to destroy us. Satan is "the deceiver of the whole world" (Revelation 12:10). Our battle is not with other people, and not with ourselves. Our battle is spiritual (Ephesians 6:12). The enemy, Satan, is described as the "accuser of our brethren" (Revelation 12:10). This scripture goes on to say that Satan accuses us before God, day and night. Accusation is so dangerous because it can use an element of truth; but it perverts the truth. Remember, the devil was an angel and he knows God's Word (Ezekiel 28:14-15: "Thou art the anointed cherub that covereth; and I have set thee so: thou wast upon the holy mountain of God; thou hast walked up and down in the midst of the stones of fire. Thou wast perfect in thy ways from the day that thou wast created, till iniquity was found in thee").

For an example, let's say someone committed adultery. The moment they agree with the unclean spirit to commit adultery Satan's kingdom begins accusing them to God. First, a member of Satan's kingdom, an unclean spirit, tempted them with adultery. And then when they fall into the act of adultery, Satan points out their sin, arguing that they should receive the penalty for the sinful act.

I image Satan screaming: "She's an adulterer! She's an adulterer! She's no good, kill her!" Did they commit adultery? Yes. Are they an adulterer? No.

Satan is presenting a one-sided argument. He omits our privilege as a King's kid to repent for adultery and be forgiven in Jesus' name. He omits the goodness God deposited inside of us when he created us in His image. He disregards the fact that even if we come from a family line of adulterers, God can remove everything in us that's not of Him, including adultery. By His grace we are still children of God, and adultery is not our identity. Nothing can change our status as a child of God. While we're cautioned not to continue sinning (Romans 6:1-2: "What shall we say then? Shall we continue in sin, that grace may abound? God forbid. How shall we, that are dead to sin, live any longer therein?"), the adulterous act doesn't have to damn our souls, as Satan would have it.

Satan already knows he's presenting a one-sided argument, but do you and I know it all the time? We agree with the evil spirit of accusation when (1) we agree with accusations directed towards us and (2) when we agree with accusations about others. Accusation sounds like this:

"You're mean!"
"God is unfair!"
"I'm stupid!"
"You/I never do anything right."

Accusation is a form of judgment. We are likely agreeing with the sin of accusation whenever we identify someone by a sin or a negative trait. The Bible outlines how we are to deal with saints that have sinful lifestyles (Matthew 18:15-20). We "speak evil of no man, to be no brawlers, but gentle, shewing all meekness unto all men" (Titus 3:2). Righteous judgment isn't condemning (Matthew 5:7: "Blessed are the merciful: for they shall obtain mercy"), **hypocritical** (Matthew 7:3: "And why beholdest thou the mote that is in thy brother's eye, but considerest not the beam that is in thine own eye?"), **shallow** (John 7:24: "Judge not according to the appearance, but judge righteous judgment") **or hasty** (Proverbs 18:13: "He that

REPLACE ACCUSATION WITH GOODNESS

answereth a matter before he heareth it, it is folly and shame unto him").

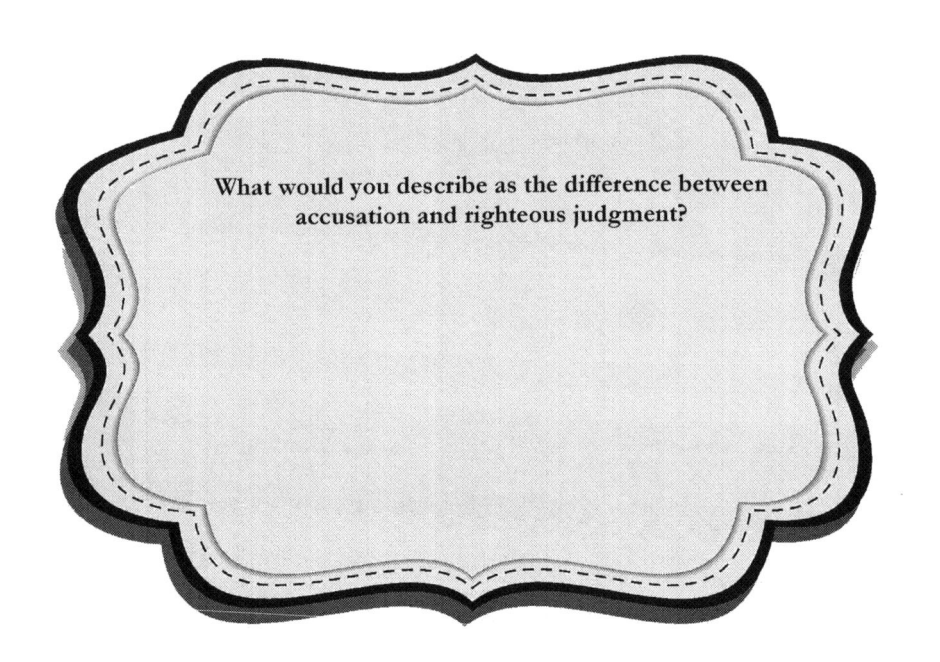

> What would you describe as the difference between accusation and righteous judgment?

The Fight

Take a moment to repent (aloud) for any accusations you may have participated with. You can say **"Father God, I repent (change my mind) for participating with the accusations against [list people including God and self if applicable]:** _____, _____, _____, _____."

Now, you can use the following FatherPa prayer model to confess an accusation deliverance prayer aloud. Say it aloud to be effective (Proverbs 18:21).

Forgiveness Ask God for forgiveness and forgive others	Father God, please forgive me for agreeing with the spirit of accusation towards _____[list person]_____. I forgive myself for agreeing with the spirit of accusation towards _____[list person]_____. Also, I forgive _____ for _____. Thank you for forgiving me. [Take time to profess forgiveness of anyone you have a problem with, especially concerning their participation with the spirit of bondage, but in other areas too. Consider whether you need to forgive God, yourself and/or others. The other person doesn't always have to be present. God forgives us as we forgive others (Mark 11:26)].
Avoid temptation	Help me not to be tested with the spirit of accusation towards _____[list person]_____ beyond what I'm able to bear. Help me resist the devil. And when I'm tempted to agree with

Replace Accusation with Goodness

	accusation, show me the way out. Show me the way of escape you promised (1 Corinthians 10:13).
Truth	Father, thank you for showing me your goodness and the goodness of myself and others because we are made in your image.
His will	I receive your goodness.
Eternal praise	You are worthy to be praised. You are the one wise God.
Rescue me	Deliver me from the spirit of accusation towards _____[list person]_____. I can't do it on my own. Please deliver me through the blood of Jesus.
Provision daily	Remind me daily that you made everyone good, desirable and approved of.
Agree with God	Thank you for delivering me from a spirit of accusation towards _____[list person]_____. You love me. I receive your love. In the name of Jesus Christ of Nazareth I pray. Amen

Very Good

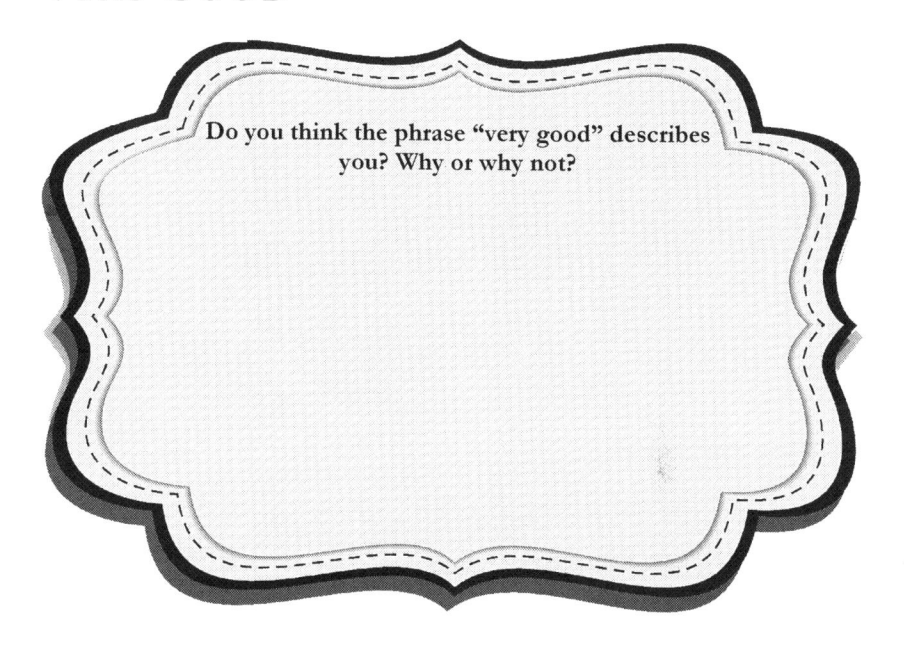

> Do you think the phrase "very good" describes you? Why or why not?

Woman of worth, YOU were created in the image of God. He created you good. The *New Oxford American Dictionary*'s definition of "good" means to be desired or approved of. God desires you, and you should desire God! It is the trick of our enemy (John 8:44: "When he speaketh a lie, he speaketh of his own: for he is a liar, and the father of it") to give you thoughts that make you feel bad, guilty or shameful. Satan is the accuser of the brethren (Rev. 12:10: "for the accuser of our brethren is cast down, which accused them before our God day and night").

In cultures around the world, and sometimes even within the church, women are continually given messages to suggest that we are somehow inadequate or less important. In the U.S. women earn $0.77 to the $1.00 a man earns for the same job. Unfortunately, this inequality extends within the church too, where women are limited in their ministry participation based solely on our gender. Lastly, consider a traditional Judaic (the religion that is in some respects the forebear of Christianity) prayer that instructs men to daily thank God for not making them a woman. This prayer certainly demonstrates a level of humanity's disdain for women.

Women must not believe we are somehow unworthy or less valuable than men. That is a lie…God made you very good (Genesis 1:31: "And God saw every thing that he had made, and, behold, it was very good"). There is no male or female in Christ (Galatians 3:28: "There is neither male nor female: for ye are all one in Christ Jesus"). God made men and women very good. Everything God made was very good. You are precious. God desires you and approves of you.

Read Genesis 1:27 and 2:21-23. When God created Eve, He made her in His image. God created Eve "very good" and with purpose. However, being "very good" does not exempt us from our ability to sin. The serpent tempted Eve to agree with him (sin). Adam and Eve sinned when they ate the forbidden fruit.

Two types of curses resulted from this violation of God's law: 1). God cursed the serpent (Satan); and 2). God cursed the act of sin. But God never cursed Adam or Eve, so we remain in the "very good" state. The two biblical references of "curse" are:

Curse = serpent (Satan)
Curse = consequences of agreeing with anything that is contrary to God's standards

The only times we read about women (or men) being cursed is as a consequence of violating God's standards (sin). This means that it is the sin that is cursed, not you or I. We only enter into a cursed state when there's sin lurking. We are still "very good"! But there's more good news; Jesus can redeem us from the curse. Jesus saves our sinful souls and teaches us how to live righteously (Galatians 3:13: "Christ hath redeemed us from the curse of the law, being made a curse for us"). Oh, how I love Jesus!

Sisters, we are "very good" because God made us that way. We don't have to prove anything to anyone. We don't have to perform or complete a special mission. We don't have to earn an award. God made you "very good" in the beginning. No one can tell you different. We are good because a good God made us. Yes, it is true that "God don't make no junk"!

> Since God describes us as very good, who or what makes us think differently at times?

When that enemy starts talking to you (through your thoughts, or through someone else), you can resist him by letting him know you are very good.

Have you ever wondered how God sees you? Here's a list of ways God describes you in Christ. Confess these truths aloud.

1. I am **Holy** (1 Corinthians 6:19-20)
2. I am a **Servant of God** (Hebrews 9:14)
3. I am a **Friend of God** (John 15:15)
4. I am a **World Changer** (Romans 8:11)
5. I am a **Child of God** (John 1:12)
6. I am **Pleasurable to God** (Ephesians 1:5)
7. I am **Accepted** (Romans 15:7)
8. I am **Known** (Jeremiah 1:5)
9. I am **Chosen** (1 Peter 2:9)
10. I am a member of a **Royal Priesthood** (1 Peter 2:9)

1. Which two of the above descriptions are most meaningful to you? Why?

_____

_____

_____

2. Look through the Bible and find two more ways you are described by God.

I am _____

I am _____

5
Pathways
Replace Uncleanness with Holiness

5 Replace Uncleanness with Holiness

For years following my divorce, I was plagued with sexual and romantic dreams. Initially I didn't know I was entertaining an unclean spirit, but I was.

As believers, we cannot allow our bodies to be used for unclean acts, even in our dreams (Galatians 5:24: "And they that are Christ's have crucified the flesh with the affections and lusts"). I thought I was in good standing with God in that area since I wasn't having intercourse in the natural realm; but remember, God looks at the heart (1 Samuel 16:7: "for *the LORD seeth* not as man seeth; for man looketh on the outward appearance, but the LORD looketh on the heart"). All of my affections belong to God (Mark 12:30: "And thou shalt love the Lord thy God with all thy heart [*Strong's* G2588—thoughts or feelings], and with all thy soul, and with all thy mind, and with all thy strength: this is the first commandment").

These recurring romantic dreams let me know I still had a spirit of sexual lust lurking somewhere in my spirit-man; in my heart. So what's the big deal? Though no one else knew about my secret dream life (actually, it wasn't a secret for long because I began to confess to trusted ladies as soon as I realized it wasn't of God), God did. It's tough for me to explain this, but there were physical consequences to agreeing with and enjoying my romantic dream life; I'd have physical ailments in the days following the dreams. I was participating with an unclean spirit.

I'm sure one of the ways the unclean spirit accessed me was through a sexual partner who was addicted to pornography (1 Corinthians 6:16: "What? know ye not that he which is joined to an harlot is one body? for two, saith he, shall be one flesh"). But there could have been other ways too—watching lewd shows, generational iniquity and so forth. In participating with the unclean spirit, God was still using me; but I was more of a vessel of dishonor (2 Tim. 2:20-22: "But in a great house there are not only vessels of gold and of silver, but also of wood and of earth; and some to honour, and some to dishonour. If a man therefore purge himself from these, he shall be a vessel unto honour, sanctified, and meet for the master's use, and prepared unto every good work. Flee also youthful lusts: but follow righteousness, faith, charity, peace, with them that call on the Lord out of a pure heart"). The more I participate with God in cleaning me up through the process of sanctification, the more He uses me for His noble purposes.

Studying and applying the principles in the book of Jude delivered me of the unclean spirit that tormented me. For the most part, it was a three-part process. First, I had to repent and start hating participation with the dreams (Galatians 5:24: "And they that are Christ's have crucified the flesh with the affections and lusts"). I got rid of everything I owned that represented any past sexual perversion—even my bed! Then, I realized and confessed that I couldn't overcome this unclean demon on my own (Jude 24), and I continually need God's help. For me, this third step was the most powerful in helping me overcome (Ephesians 2:8-9: "For by grace are ye saved through faith; and that not of yourselves: it is the gift of God: Not of works, lest any man should boast").

To this day, every night, I break evil soul ties and ask God to keep me from falling. He is faithful. Thank you Lord! Overcoming the unclean spirit has been a major accomplishment on my road to righteousness, and I have so much peace in my life as a result—no more guilt and shame.

The Fight

The unclean spirit gives us carnal desires and affections when we participate with it. Sexual immorality is just one example of how an unclean spirit can manifest. Unclean spirits fulfill the lust of the flesh, as seen in Galatians 5:19-21: "Now the works of the flesh are manifest, which are these; Adultery, fornication, uncleanness, lasciviousness, Idolatry, witchcraft, hatred, variance, emulations, wrath, strife, seditions, heresies, Envyings, murders, drunkenness, revellings, and such like: of the which I tell you before, as I have also told you in time past, that they which do such things shall not inherit the kingdom of God."

We know we're being tempted by an unclean spirit when we feel driven to do something; when I start thinking "I've got to have this or do this now!" For this reason, unclean spirits are most easily identified within addictions and sexual perversion. Evil spirits like rejection, fear and unforgiveness generally dwell within our minds and hearts. However, the unclean spirits tend to dwell within the lusts/desires of the body and thought life. The object of an unclean desire doesn't have to be something "bad", only something we prioritize before God. We can lust after food, sleep, education, drugs, sex, alcohol, relationships, etc. Do you think about anything more often than godly principles? Do you desire anything more than God's will? Do you depend on something or someone before God? Are you spending more of your time/resources on fulfilling your desires, in place of pleasing God? Yes, God does give us the desires of our hearts, but it will be a gift from Him that aligns with God's will, in His time. God gives us gifts that "maketh rich, and he addeth no sorrow with it" (Proverbs 10:22).

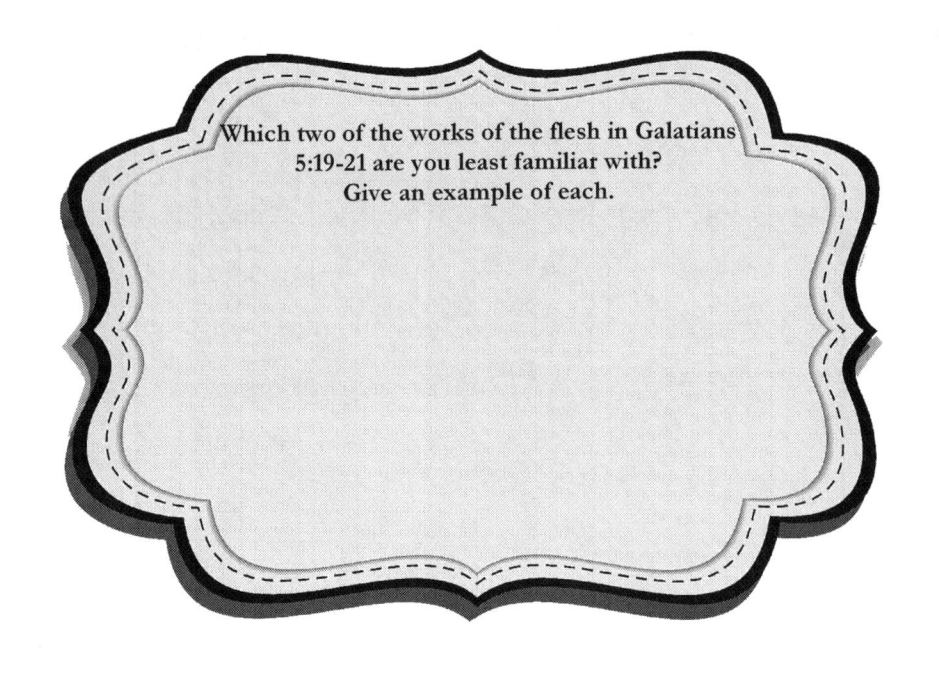

> Which two of the works of the flesh in Galatians 5:19-21 are you least familiar with? Give an example of each.

The Greek definition of "unclean" is impure and foul. Like a white rag that gets dirty when we use it to scrub oven grime, uncleanness is a product of using our faculties (body, mind and emotions) to fulfill ungodly desires and affections. God has given us power over unclean spirits, and we can choose whether we will participate with the lust they bring (Luke 10:19: "Behold, I give unto you power to tread on serpents and scorpions, and over all the power of the enemy: and nothing shall by any means hurt you"). In doing so, we become vessels of dishonor; requiring a thorough wash from the Word, Jesus Christ. In fact, only our participation with Jesus Christ can make us vessels of honor, because our righteousness is as filthy rags (Isaiah 64:6: "But we are all as an unclean thing, and all our righteousnesses are as filthy rags; and we all do fade as a leaf; and our iniquities, like the wind, have taken us away"). We, through faith and action, get to choose whether we want to be vessels of dishonor or honor, for the Master's use (2 Tim. 2:20-22: "But in a great house there are not only vessels of gold and of silver, but also of wood and of earth; and some to honour, and some to dishonour. If a man therefore purge himself from these, he shall be a vessel unto honour, sanctified, and meet for the master's use, and prepared unto every good work. Flee also youthful lusts: but follow righteousness, faith, charity, peace, with them that call on the Lord out of a pure heart").

The God-Wash

Take a moment to repent (aloud) for any uncleanness you may have participated with. You can say **"Father God, I repent (change my mind) for participating with the following unclean acts: _____,**

_____, _____,
_____."

Now, you can follow the following three practical steps (from the book of Jude) to get rid of unclean spirits attached to persons, places or things.

STEP 1: REESTABLISH THE FEAR OF GOD IN YOUR LIFE (Jude 23: "and others save with fear"). The Greek definition of fear in this verse means deep reverential accountability to God or Christ. In other words, God hates sin, so we need to stop sinning when we recognize it. Develop a perfect hatred for the lust object of the unclean spirit.

Believe it and say it aloud whenever you're tempted; **"get away from me you unclean spirit of** _____ **[drunkenness, sexual perversion, etc.]. I crucify the flesh** [carnal nature] **with its passions and desires** (Galatians 5:24) **in the name of Jesus Christ of Nazareth."**

STEP 2: HATE THE SINFUL GARMENTS (Jude 23: "hating even the garment spotted by the flesh"). This means you may have to **get rid of some stuff.** Some people need to get rid of old undergarments, old gifts, or even an old bed as I did. This could also include leaving an unhealthy relationship. Get rid of anything that symbolizes the unclean lust or affection. If you hate something, you don't keep it around. If your computer caused you to sin, you may need to get rid of it and maybe get a new one when you're ready.

STEP 3: RELY ON GOD (Jude 24: "Now unto him that is able to keep you from falling, and present you faultless before the presence of his glory with exceeding joy"). Do your part, but remember you can't do it alone, without Him. Jesus, by the power of the Holy Spirit is the one who's going to deliver you.

Read the Bible, pray, thank him…every day! He is able to keep you from falling, but you've got to stay connected and obedient to Him. He's able to present you faultless, but you've got to stay connected and obedient to Him. He's able to give you exceeding joy, but you've got to stay connected and obedient to Him.

Believe and say **"Father, keep me from falling into participating with the unclean spirit of _____ [drunkenness, sexual perversion, etc.] in Jesus' name. Thank you Father."**

Pathways to God and His Goodness (Holiness and Righteousness)

More than anything God wants a relationship with you, and He wants to bless your socks off! But getting to this will require holy and righteous living. God is holy and He calls you to be the same (1 Peter 1:16: "Be ye holy; for I am holy"—none of which can be accomplished without God). He desires that you become more like Him than you were last week, last year, yesterday. Yes, He is love and she who abides in God, and God in her are blessed abundantly (John 15:5: "I am the vine, ye are the branches: He that abideth in me, and I in him, the same bringeth forth much fruit: for without me ye can do nothing").

God created us good, and He has good plans for us (Jeremiah 29:11: "For I know the thoughts that I think toward you, saith the Lord, thoughts of peace, and not of evil, to give you an expected end"). Holiness and righteousness are the pathways to receive God's goodness.

Sin, on the other hand, can separate us from God's goodness (Isaiah 59:2: "But your iniquities have separated between you and your God, and your sins have hid *his* face from you, that he will not hear"). Sure, God will extend grace and mercy to whomever He will, even people who aren't holy and righteous (Romans 9:18: "Therefore hath he mercy on whom he will have mercy, and whom he will he hardeneth"). But, to be a covenant daughter, to receive the abundant life Christ came to give (John 10:10: "The thief cometh not, but for to steal, and to kill, and to destroy: I am come that they might have life, and that they might have it more abundantly"), God requires holiness and righteousness. Sister girl, if you want to receive all the goodness of God, you have to be holy and righteous. That should be the goal that we strive for. God loves and aids us. He shapes us to His purpose, because none of us are holy without him (Rev. 15:4: "for thou only art holy"). They are goals to strive for.

1. **What or who comes to mind when you think of the words holy and righteous? Why?**

_____

_____

2. **Do you consider yourself holy and righteous? Why or why not?**

_____

_____

What Is Holiness?

Holiness describes our God, and it should be a GOAL of every daughter. Day by day we fellowship with God to become less sinful and more holy, in thought and deed. It is a continual, lifelong process to "work out your own salvation with fear and trembling" (Philippians 2:12). We maintain holiness through grace and mercy (knowledge, repentance and constant prayer).

To be holy means to be set apart for God's purpose. It can also mean being morally and spiritually excellent; without sin. It is a matter of the heart. 1 Samuel 16:7 reads, "But the LORD said unto Samuel, Look not on his countenance, or on the height of his stature; because I have refused him: for *the LORD seeth* not as man seeth; for man looketh on the outward appearance, but the LORD looketh on the heart." For this reason even some ministers may not get into the kingdom of heaven (Matthew 7:21-23: "Not every one that saith unto me, Lord, Lord, shall enter into the kingdom of heaven; but he that doeth the will of my Father which is in heaven. Many will say to me in that day, Lord, Lord, have we not prophesied in thy name? and in thy name have cast out devils? and in thy name done many wonderful works? And then will I profess unto them, I never knew you: depart from me, ye that work iniquity"). Jesus is a just and righteous judge because He doesn't judge by what we see; he judges our heart, our inner thoughts and motives. It is Jesus who will judge believers, not Father God (John 5:22: "For the Father judgeth no man, but hath committed all judgment unto the Son").

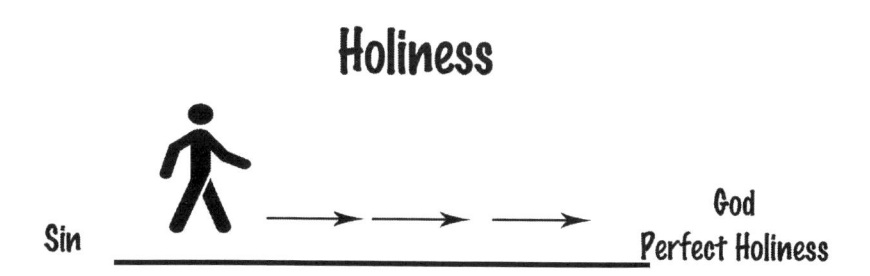

Holiness

Sin → → → God Perfect Holiness

WHAT IS RIGHTEOUSNESS?

Righteousness is a GIFT through faith in Christ (Philippians 3:9: "not having mine own righteousness, which is of the law, but that which is through the faith of Christ, the righteousness which is of God by faith"). Righteousness is doing the will of the Father, not your own will. Apart from God, we know that "all our righteousness are as filthy rags" (Isaiah 64:6). We become righteous when we realize all of our holy thinking and living doesn't even come close to meeting God's standards. However, we acknowledge that God still requires us to be righteous (Romans 8:4: "that the righteousness of the law might be fulfilled in us, who walk not after the flesh, but after the Spirit"). At this point we have no choice but to ask God for help, and accept His righteous gift of redemption through Jesus' death and resurrection. We receive God's righteousness as our own. Lord, thank you for giving me your righteousness so that I can commune with you holy God!

Righteousness

Sin — Human's best holiness efforts

We need help to move any further

Gift of righteousness through Jesus Christ

God
Perfect Holiness

3. Explain holiness in your own words.

4. Explain righteousness in your own words.

5. What do you do when you are living holy and you miss the mark (sin)?

REPLACE UNCLEANNESS WITH HOLINESS

6. Can you fulfill God's righteousness on your own?

7. Is a godly woman righteous and holy? Why or why not?

6

Personal Connection
Replace Occultism with Relationship

6 Replace Occultism with a Personal Relationship with God

Secret Societies

I first heard the term "occultism" during a training session at Be in Health (BIH) in Thomaston, GA. We went through an extensive list of occult practices, whereby I repented for my personal involvement and involvement in my generations (parents, grandparents, etc.) (Leviticus 26:40-42: "If they shall confess their iniquity, and the iniquity of their fathers, with their trespass which they trespassed against me, and that also they have walked contrary unto me; And that I also have walked contrary unto them, and have brought them into the land of their enemies; if then their uncircumcised hearts be humbled, and they then accept of the punishment of their iniquity: Then will I remember my covenant with Jacob, and also my covenant with Isaac, and also my covenant with Abraham will I remember; and I will remember the land"). I was fine with repenting for everything on the list, except my membership in a sorority. You see, not only was I a member, but I was a former chapter president.

Following our ministry session I marched up to the minister to inform her that she was wrong about sororities being occult. I explained to her that my sorority was dedicated to community service, and I began listing all the wonderful godly things we were doing. The minister explained to me that the major problem with sororities was the "secret" element (like freemansory), and I think she also mentioned something about rituals too. Still, she could tell I wasn't convinced so she ended our discussion by informing me that the Bible said I had to be convinced in my own heart; it wasn't counted against me as sin if I hadn't been convicted (James 4:17: "Therefore to him that knoweth to do good, and doeth *it* not, to him it is sin").

That was the very scriptural and appropriate response from that Be in Health minister. But I had a couple of sistah girls who'd overheard our discussion, and grabbed me to insist the sorority was evil. They told me to watch *The Truth behind the Black Church* by G. Craig Lewis. And when I returned home from the ministry training, I did exactly that. I bought and watched the DVD. Will Ford presented a side to Greek life that I'd never considered: the fact that the sorority I belonged to revolved around a Greek goddess, and in much of the sorority's ceremony we mentioned the goddess. Yes, a scripture or two was read, but the Greek goddess was definitely the focus. I began thinking about some of the sorority chants, philosophies and songs that I felt uncomfortable reciting as a Believer ("I am the master of my soul," "I'll always be a member," "lifetime commitment," "I pledge my heart to the sorority," and the like). All of this led me to study my Bible and eventually to my decision to renounce the sorority.

The most simplistic definition I can give is "occultism is deception." Below, I've outlined the five characteristics of occultism I discovered through scripture and the Holy Spirit. One or more of these characteristics can be evident in all types of occultism, not just secret societies. However, my involvement in the sorority included all five characteristics.

(1) Occultism offers an alternative to Christ. The truth is, Jesus is the answer—as John 14:6 puts it, "Jesus saith unto him, I am the way, the truth, and the life." I thought I'd be helping my community by joining the sorority. However, Jesus is the savior of the world/our community…not me or any secret society. This is not to say one should never try to help one's community. However, it does mean that our ultimate reliance for change should be on Jesus, not a secret society. Some secret societies even go as far as describing themselves as "the light of the world." This is blasphemous.

(2) Occultism incorporates idolatry. The truth is, we should have no gods in the presence of the only true God. Deuteronomy 5:7 states, "Thou shalt have none other gods before [*Strong's* H664: in the face of] me." While the sorority I joined claims to be founded on Christian principles, imagery and rituals concerning the Greek goddess Minerva were standard practice. This sort of deity imagery is common within other secret societies too.

This is idolatry. The Greek definition of "idol" in *Strong's* is "an image for worship or a heathen god." An idol can also be anything we substitute for the one and true living God. As believers, we don't esteem another deity in God's presence. We can't worship God + another deity. 1 Corinthians 10:21 explains, "Ye cannot drink the cup of the Lord, and the cup of devils: ye cannot be partakers of the Lord's table, and of the table of devils."

(3) Occultism mixes the truth with lies. The truth is, we're called to separate ourselves from lies. Occultism can acknowledge Christ as one way to salvation, while acknowledging other "ways" too. Anything that offers an alternative route to salvation, outside of God's Word, is a lie: "A little leaven leaveneth the whole lump," (Galatians 5:9); "Be ye not unequally yoked together with unbelievers: for what fellowship hath righteousness with unrighteousness? and what communion hath light with darkness?" (2 Corinthians 6:14); "Wherefore come out from among them, and be ye separate, saith the Lord, and touch not the unclean *thing*; and I will receive you" (2 Corinthians 6:17).

This doesn't mean we can't interact with unbelievers; but we shouldn't bind ourselves to such things. We don't need occult practices (or organizations) to accomplish God's will in our lives. God instructs us not to forsake the assembly of the righteous; not worldly groups (Hebrews 10:25). I thank God for the gift of repentance concerning my membership in the sorority, and for sweet forgiveness in Jesus!

(4) Occultism creates ungodly covenants. The truth is, God tells us not to make oaths: "But I say unto you, Swear not at all; neither by heaven; for it is God's throne" (Matthew 5:34). Also, ceremony, rituals and oaths have spiritual implications—know what you're saying and getting into (Proverbs 18:21: "Death and life are in the power of the tongue: and they that love it shall eat the fruit thereof"). Secret societies are dangerous because you don't have an opportunity to truly research the oaths/pledges before you're expected to make them. You're given information and expected to accept it, immediately, in order to join the group.

(5) Occultism shows evidence of providing us benefits. The truth is, the devil is deceiving—"For there shall arise false christs and false prophets and shall show great signs and wonders, insomuch that, if it were possible, they shall deceive the very elect" (Matthew 24:24). People join secret societies because of the benefits they promise. Secret societies promise a sisterhood that can be very appealing to individuals who may feel like a "black sheep" in some way. They promise an elite international network that can help you get a good job and have more fun.

Believers need more discernment in joining social organizations. Don't trust organizations just because they incorporate a few scriptures into their philosophies. Even the devil knows scripture, and he recited scripture when he tempted Jesus in the wilderness.

My motivation in joining the sorority was to join a group of women who were committed to leadership and community service. In trying to do something "good" I got tangled up with sin. I was deceived. And though I don't believe God counted my involvement as sin, there were natural consequences to my involvement with the occult.

Be in Health research describes occultism as a block to our relationship with God. I've found this to be true—I had trouble reading and retaining His Word in my heart. Now, since I've renounced the occultism, I find it hard to stop studying God's Word. My vow to the sorority was a block to my access to the Kingdom of God to a large degree, as is all occultism (Galatians 5:19-21: "Now the works of the flesh are manifest, which are these; Adultery, fornication, uncleanness, lasciviousness, idolatry, witchcraft, hatred, variance, emulations, wrath, strife, seditions, heresies, envyings, murders, drunkenness, revellings, and such like: of the which I tell you before, as I have also told you in time past, that they which do such things shall not inherit the kingdom of God"). It hindered my ability to understand and apply godly spiritual truths, rendering me powerless in spiritual warfare (John 8:32: "And ye shall know the truth, and the truth shall make you free"). Knowing and applying God's truth is deliverance! I have greater peace and better health since getting rid of the occultism I recognize in my life. Occultism can block us from God's truth and from our deliverance.

Defining Occultism

Occultism gives us the illusion that there's something else, other than following Christ, we have to do to obtain an abundant life; it is a work of the flesh. It offers you "the secret" to your healing and happiness. On the contrary, the way of Christ is not a secret to those who follow Him and study His Word. The dictionary meaning of occultism is "of, involving, or relating to supernatural, mystical, or magical powers or phenomena; beyond the range of ordinary knowledge or experience."

Pharmekia

The Greek word for "witchcraft" in Galatians 5:20 is pharmekia ("pharmacy"), which means medication, and by extension magic (literally or figuratively). Drugs, legal and illegal, can be considered a form of occultism, depending on your motivation for taking the drug. BIH offers a few questions to consider in determining the motivation in taking prescription drugs, "Has the person asked God for healing? Are they working on changing the sinful behavior that may have triggered the disease in the first place? Has the medication become the goal so that they don't have to turn to God? We all know that some medications also so alter a person's consciousness that they are literally in another reality. This would be of the occult just as much as a drunken alcoholic state or a state of bliss achieved by some ungodly meditations would be."

This is not to say that we should never use prescription or over-the-counter drugs, but they shouldn't be our salvation plan. "For the kingdom of God is not meat and drink; but righteousness, and peace, and joy in the Holy Ghost" (Romans 14:17). In non-emergency instances, seek God before the physician. Seek God and His Word before Google. Even in emergencies, pray on your way to the hospital. Prescription drugs can be necessary at times, but realize it's not God's best plan for you. Drugs have side effects that cause other diseases, but God's deliverance doesn't—it's all good (Proverbs 10:22: "The blessing of the LORD, it maketh rich, and he addeth no sorrow with it")!

This same occult principle can be applied to anything we digest for deliverance and health. The devil doesn't care what it is, as long as he has you in bondage. I used to be addicted to vitamins and supplements; taking a certain vitamin for this symptom, and another one for that symptom. I was taking vitamins every three hours to "maintain" comfort and "optimal health." Thank God He showed me that the enemy was giving my body physical manifestations (symptoms) to get me hooked. I was delivered when I learned to submit to God and resist the devil (James 4:7). The devil loves trying to get me to fight his temptations with occultism, his solution. Thank God I'm learning the truth and the enemy's tactics.

SCIENCES, PROCESSES AND OTHER SPIRITUAL PRACTICES

Christ never instructed us to study the stars, recite mantras or access any spiritual realm outside of Him. In fact, He describes such practices as sin and an abomination to Him. Deuteronomy 18: 10-12 reads, "There shall not be found among you any one that maketh his son or his daughter to pass through the fire, or that useth divination [the practice of seeking knowledge of the future or the unknown by supernatural means], or an observer of times, or an enchanter, or a witch. Or a charmer, or a consulter with familiar spirits, or a wizard, or a necromancer. For all that do these things are an abomination unto the Lord: and because of these abominations the Lord thy God doth drive them out from before thee." Deuteronomy 4:19 further explains occult modalities by saying "and lest thou lift up thine eyes unto heaven, and when thou seest the sun, and the moon, and the stars, [even] all the host of heaven, shouldest be driven to worship them, and serve them, which the LORD thy God hath divided unto all nations under the whole heaven." Occult practices include any art or entity that operates independently from God to give you some type of an advantage. These practices push us further away from the Lord and His Kingdom.

Whenever we're introduced to something that is described as "spiritual," we need to pump the breaks to determine if it is godly or occult. Ask yourself:
- "Is the root of this practice from some other man or

deity?"
- "Is Jesus just one of the acceptable gods in this practice?"
- "Am I doing this even though I can't find a biblical example of it?"
- "Am I trying to gain benefits, access, or information apart from the plan God laid out in the Bible?"

Pray about everything, and if you answer yes to any of the aforementioned questions, the practice is very likely occult. Occult practices are inherently wrong, designed to aid or "help" God, as if God and His ways aren't sufficient. New Age practices are a good example of occultism. According to Wikipedia, the new age movement is "characterised by a holistic view of the cosmos, a belief in an emergent Age of Aquarius—from which the movement gets its name—an emphasis on self-spirituality and the authority of the self, a focus on healing (particularly with alternative medicine), a belief in channeling, and an adoption of a 'New Age science' that makes use of elements of what adherents call the new physics."

Other common examples of occult practices include: horoscopes, astrology, tarot and psychic readings, necromancy (consulting the dead), yoga, pilates, channeling, séances, automatic writing, interpreting omens, divination, channeling spirits, reflexology, karate and other martial arts, kundalini spirit, false prophesy, angel worship, and many more.

Summing It Up

Occultism can be difficult to discern, because it is sometimes taught and practiced in Christian churches. It's important we learn God's Word for ourselves, so we'll know what to accept and participate in. Of course learning God's Word can be challenging, until we get rid of the occultism. Don't readily believe signs and wonders, because the devil has some power to manifest those too (2 Thessalonians 2:9: "*Even him, whose coming is after the working of Satan with all power and signs and lying wonders*"). Be in Health's measure is, "If God didn't do it in the Word, if Jesus didn't do it in the Word, then we don't do it."

Occultism is a lie; a pretender, a phony, a knock-off. It is Satan's kingdom pretending to be the Kingdom of God. For a brief period, it can give you the results you want; but eventually it always leads to greater bondage. The devil hates you, and he only comes to "steal, and to kill, and to destroy" (John 10:10). Occultism steals our peace, time, money, relationships with ourselves and others, and, most importantly, our relationships with God. Jesus is the only way (John 14:6: "Jesus saith unto him, I am the way, the truth, and the life").

The Fight

Acts 19:19-20 instructs us on how to deal with occultism in our lives. "And many that believed came, and confessed, and shewed their deeds. Many of them also which used curious arts brought their books together, and burned them before all men: and they counted the price of them, and found it fifty thousand pieces of silver. So mightily grew the word of God and prevailed." The New Testament church repented and burned the occult books, so that the word of God would have power. As we repent for the occultism in our lives, and get rid of the occult paraphernalia, God's power can increase in our lives too! Take a moment to repent (aloud) for any occultism you may have participated with. You can say, **"Father God, I repent (change my mind) for participating with the** following occult practices: _____,

_____, _____,

_____."

Now, you can use the following FatherPa prayer model to confess an occultism deliverance prayer aloud.

Forgiveness Ask God for forgiveness and forgive others	Father God, please forgive me for agreeing with the spirit of occultism by _____[insert type(s) of occultism]_____. I forgive myself for agreeing with the spirit of occultism by _____[insert type(s) of occultism]_____. Also, I forgive _____ for _____. Thank you for forgiving me. [Take time to profess forgiveness of anyone you have a problem with, especially concerning their participation with the spirit of bondage, but in other areas too. Consider whether you need to forgive God, yourself and/or others. The other person doesn't always have to be present. God forgives us as we forgive others (Mark 11:26)].
Avoid temptation	Help me not to be tested with the spirit of occultism by _____[insert type of occultism]_____ beyond what I'm able to bear. Help me resist the devil. And when I'm tempted to agree with bondage, show me the way out. Show me the way of escape you promised (1 Corinthians 10:13).
Truth	Father, thank you for setting me free.
His will	I receive your freedom.

Eternal praise	You are worthy to be praised. You are the one wise God.
Rescue me	Deliver me from the spirit of occultism by _____[insert type (s) of occultism]_____. I can't do it on my own. Please deliver me through the blood of Jesus.
Provision daily	Remind me daily that you are the way, the truth and the life.
Agree with God	Thank you for delivering me from a spirit of occultism by _____[insert type(s) of occultism]_____. You love me. I receive your love. In the name of Jesus Christ of Nazareth I pray. Amen

Your Personal Connection with the Godhead

God is with us on our life journey, teaching us to be holy. Jesus ripped the veil that separated us from God (Mark 15:38: "And the veil of the temple was rent in twain from the top to the bottom"), so that now we can talk directly to Him whenever we want. We go boldly—not timidly—to His throne of grace with all of our desires, needs, thoughts and requests (Hebrews 4:16: "Let us therefore come boldly unto the throne of grace, that we may obtain mercy, and find grace to help in time of need"). Jesus showed us the way, instructing us to pray **directly** to the Father in Jesus' name (John 16:23: "And in that day ye shall ask me nothing. Verily, verily, I say unto you, Whatsoever ye shall ask the Father in my name, he will give it you"). Bring all of your hopes, doubts, desires and questions to your Father in prayer. Our Father owns the cattle on a thousand hills (Psalm 50:10: "For every beast of the forest is mine, and the cattle upon a thousand hills")! Everything good comes from our Father (James 1:17: "Every good gift and every perfect gift is from above, and cometh down from the Father"). He can supply all of your needs. He is listening and He cares.

> Have you ever asked someone else to meet your need, before going to God? Why?

In the Bible

PRAYER

Read 1 Samuel 1. Remember Hannah, the married childless woman who was tormented by her husband's other wife? What did she do in response to her situation? She prayed…directly to God. She didn't ask anyone else to pray for her (though at times prayer help is appropriate); she "prayed unto the Lord, and wept sore" (1 Sam. 1:10) And in verse 19, we see that God answered her prayers and gave her a son.

Hannah **ask**ed God for a blessing. Today, our requests are directed towards God the Father in Jesus' name.

Make three requests to your Father God, in Jesus' name:

1. _____

2. _____

3. _____

TOUCH JESUS, FAITHFULLY

Read Luke 8:43-48. The woman with the issue of blood fought her way through a crowd of people to touch Jesus' garment and she was made whole. Jesus commended her efforts, saying, "Daughter, be of good comfort: thy faith hath made thee whole; go in peace" (Luke 8:48).

The woman with the issue of blood **touched** Jesus, **faithfully**. Jesus is described in the Bible as "the Word of God." Reading, believing and confessing Bible scriptures are ways we can touch Jesus like the woman with the issue of blood.

List three of your favorite Bible scriptures and read them aloud.

1. _____

2. _____

3. _____

ACCEPT SALVATION

Remember the woman at the well in **John 4:6-28**? It wasn't customary for Jewish men to talk with Samaritan women, but Jesus did. Also, Jesus knew the woman was a sinner, a likely outcast of her own people, yet Jesus still decided to reveal Himself to her. Jesus welcomed the fornicating Samaritan woman to salvation in Him.

The Samaritan woman **accept**ed God's invitation for salvation. The Holy Spirit helps and directs us in living godly lives through Jesus (John 16:13: "Howbeit when He, the Spirit of truth, is come, He will guide you into all truth: for he shall not speak of himself; but whatsoever he shall hear, that shall he speak: and he will shew you things to come. He shall glorify me [Jesus]: for he shall receive of mine, and shall shew it unto you"). The Holy Spirit enables us to accept salvation through Jesus.

Have you accepted Father God's gift to humanity, salvation through His Son Jesus Christ? Jesus came in the flesh and died for you and me so that our sins can be forgiven and we can be reconciled to our Father. If you'd like to accept Jesus as the Lord of your life, believe and say the following sample confession aloud.

I believe Jesus Christ is the only Son of God. I believe he came in the flesh as a man. I believe he was crucified for my sins, but he rose again in three days. I invite Jesus to live in my heart, and I accept his sacrifice for me.

Father God I am willing to turn from all my sins. Please forgive me of all my sins in Jesus' name. Thank you God for saving me and for forgiving me of all my sins. God, help me to live an abundant life that is pleasing to you. Thank you Father that you've heard me.

God saw value in these three women. They were women of worth to Him! Just as these three women communicated directly with God, you too can go to Him anytime you want or need. These three women demonstrated three ways to connect with God through, prayer, touch and salvation. I encourage you to connect with God in these three areas too!

Meditate on the following scriptures about connecting with God through requests, the Word, and salvation.

Prayer
1. **Psalm 145:18**- The Lord is nigh unto all them that call upon him, to all that call upon him in truth.
2. **1 Chronicles 16:11**- Seek the Lord and his strength, seek his face continually.
3. **Psalm 4:1**- Hear me when I call, O God of my righteousness: thou hast enlarged me when I was in distress; have mercy upon me, and hear my prayer.
4. **Matthew 7:11**- If ye then, being evil, know how to give good gifts unto your children, how much more shall your Father which is in heaven give good things to them that ask him?

5. **Proverbs 15:29**- The Lord is far from the wicked: but he heareth the prayer of the righteous.
6. **Luke 6:12**- And it came to pass in those days, that he went out into a mountain to pray, and continued all night in prayer to God.
7. **Philippians 4:6**- Be careful for nothing; but in every thing by prayer and supplication with thanksgiving let your requests be made known unto God.
8. **Romans 8:26**- Likewise the Spirit also helpeth our infirmities: for we know not what we should pray for as we ought: but the Spirit itself maketh intercession for us with groanings which cannot be uttered.
9. **James 4:3**- Ye ask, and receive not, because ye ask amiss, that ye may consume it upon your lusts.
10. **James 5:16**- Confess your faults one to another, and pray one for another, that ye may be healed. The effectual fervent prayer of a righteous man availeth much.

Touch Jesus (Jesus is described as the Word of God which includes the Holy Bible)
1. **Joshua 1:8** - This book of the law shall not depart out of thy mouth; but thou shalt meditate therein day and

night, that thou mayest observe to do according to all that is written therein: for then thou shalt make thy way prosperous, and then thou shalt have good success.

2. **2 Timothy 3:16-17**, All scripture [is] given by inspiration of God, and [is] profitable for doctrine, for reproof, for correction, for instruction in righteousness: That the man of God may be perfect, throughly furnished unto all good works.

3. **Matthew 4:4** - But he answered and said, It is written, Man shall not live by bread alone, but by every word that proceedeth out of the mouth of God.

4. **Romans 15:4** - For whatsoever things were written aforetime were written for our learning, that we through patience and comfort of the scriptures might have hope.

5. **1 Peter 2:2** - As newborn babes, desire the sincere milk of the word, that ye may grow thereby:

6. **John 1:1** - In the beginning was the Word, and the Word was with God, and the Word was God.

7. **2 Timothy 2:15** - Study to shew thyself approved unto God, a workman that needeth not to be ashamed, rightly dividing the word of truth.

8. **John 15:7** - If ye abide in me, and my words abide in you, ye shall ask what ye will, and it shall be done unto you.
9. **Psalms 119:18** - Open thou mine eyes, that I may behold wondrous things out of thy law.
10. **Psalms 119:105** - Thy word [is] a lamp unto my feet, and a light unto my path.

Accept Christ
1. **Romans 10:9** - That if thou shalt confess with thy mouth the Lord Jesus, and shalt believe in thine heart that God hath raised him from the dead, thou shalt be saved.
2. **John 14:6** - Jesus saith unto him, I am the way, the truth, and the life: no man cometh unto the Father, but by me.
3. **Romans 10:13** - For whosoever shall call upon the name of the Lord shall be saved.
4. **Romans 6:23** - For the wages of sin [is] death; but the gift of God [is] eternal life through Jesus Christ our Lord.

5. **John 3:16** - For God so loved the world, that he gave his only begotten Son, that whosoever believeth in him should not perish, but have everlasting life.
6. **John 1:12** - But as many as received him, to them gave he power to become the sons of God, [even] to them that believe on his name:
7. **1 John 1:9**- If we confess our sins, he is faithful and just to forgive us our sins, and to cleanse us from all unrighteousness.
8. **Romans 5:8**- But God commendeth his love toward us, in that, while we were yet sinners, Christ died for us.
9. **Ephesians 2:8-9**- For by grace are ye saved through faith; and that not of yourselves: it is the gift of God: Not of works, lest any man should boast.
10. **John 3:17**- For God sent not his Son into the world to condemn the world; but that the world through him might be saved.

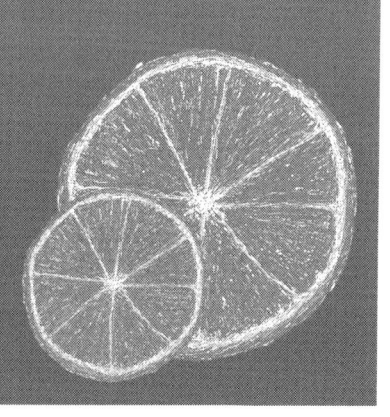

7 Healthy You

7 Healthy You

Jesus Juice helps us grow wholly; spirit, soul and body. So far, we've reviewed several lessons about our spirituality. And I've done my best to feed your soul. Now let's talk about our body.

If you've sincerely and prayerfully completed lessons 1-6, God promises you better health. Why? Because your soul is prospering and 3 John 1:2 tells us that God desires us to prosper and be in health, *as our soul prospers*. Remember, our soul includes our minds, our emotions and our desires.

One of the Greek definitions for the word "health" (G5199—*hygiaino*) in this text is "be true in doctrine" and the other is to "be well in body." If we are true in doctrine, we will likely be well in our body. Our bodies were designed by God to respect His principles. Psalm 139:14 explains "I will praise thee; for I am fearfully and wonderfully made: marvellous are thy works; and that my soul knoweth right well". The Greek word for "fearfully" in this text means reverentially. Again, our bodies are designed to respect God's principles.

Root Causes to Disease

Dr. Henry Wright, in the book *A More Excellent Way*, explains that 80% of all incurable diseases have a spiritual root cause. *A More Excellent Way* can help you pinpoint the exact spiritual root cause for an incurable disease you may have. For example, the root cause of lupus is self-hatred. After I received some Jesus Juice victory over the spirit of self-hatred, my lupus symptoms disappeared and haven't returned in five years!

In his teachings, Dr. Wright explains that spiritual roots don't always have to come from our direct agreement with sin, it could also be passed down from our parents and generations (and sometimes your husband in certain instances). Also, remember a spiritual root cause is believed to be responsible for 80% of diseases, so that leaves 20% that do not have a spiritual root cause. In any event, we can stay encouraged to know that God "forgiveth all thine iniquities; who healeth all thy diseases" (Psalm 103:3).

This book, *Jesus Juice for Health and Freedom*, takes some of the guess work out of how to get and stay free from agreeing with evil spirits. Once we've been delivered, we can then speak healing to our bodies in the name of Jesus Christ of Nazareth! But sometimes we don't have to speak healing to our bodies. I've found that sometimes the only thing needed for healing is repentance (change your mind) about agreeing with an evil spirit. This was the case with my lupus symptoms.

I was diagnosed with lupus discoid around 2004. Lupus is an autoimmune disease; a disease where the body attacks itself. In my case, lupus discoid primarily affected my scalp with large open legions. Through my healing, and through *A More Excellent Way*, I've come to realize that my body was just following my spirituality. The legions were a physical manifestation of what I'd been doing to myself spiritually. Once I agreed with God that self-hatred was a sin, and made a conscious effort to stop entertaining it (in my mind and actions), the lupus symptoms ceased.

Prior to my miraculous healing, I'd been receiving prescription steroid shots to treat the legions. The shots worked well at first, but eventually they became ineffective.

My doctor recommended that I increase the frequency of the shots to help deal with the inflammation. He also cautioned me about the side effects of the shots, including a possible deformity to the shape of my head. No thanks! I decided to try a few natural remedies which were also effective initially, but they eventually too stopped working.

Initially, I was appalled by the suggestion that lupus had anything to do with self-hatred. And I definitely didn't think it was a problem for me! I didn't even know self-hatred was a sin even though I'd been a Christian for several years. God has blessed me with many talents, and I'd say I'm average to above average concerning physical attractiveness. So, how was I agreeing with self-hatred? For me, mostly it was in my thoughts. All daylong I meditated on how awful a person I was for xyz. I was extremely hard on myself whenever I made mistakes or I disappointed others. God has brought me a long way though, and I'm learning how to see myself as God sees me. Now, I aim to please Him first in all things. I know that I am the apple of God's eye, and that I'm fearfully and wonderfully made!

I try to be super sensitive about presenting my story, because I don't want anyone to come off of prescribed medicine without their doctor's oversight. Withdrawal from medications can have serious side effects and it may take some time for you to become free in some areas. Pray, and get confirmation from your doctor.

Resisting the Devil

Once we've been set free, we've got to know how to resist the devil and his army in order to stay free.

Remember my testimony about how God wondrously delivered me from food sensitivities, and how I was so bound by food sensitivities that I could only eat sweet potatoes? Well, as soon as God delivered me, I began eating everything I could find (I've got the extra weight to prove it ;-)). But even after I'd been delivered and was able to enjoy food again, the devil continues to periodically tempt me in that area. The evil spirit will periodically tempt me to see whether I am truly filled with the Word of God (Matthew 12:43-44: "When the unclean spirit is gone out of a man, he walketh through dry places, seeking rest, and findeth none. Then he saith, I will return into my house from whence I came out; and when he is come, he findeth *it* empty, swept, and garnished").

A couple of years ago I decided to participate in my church's annual three-week Daniel fast. I did well on the fast, but whoa did I start experiencing problems when the fast ended. I started breaking out in hives when I ate certain foods. This was especially troubling because I'd never experienced these symptoms before. I'd experienced other problems with food sensitivities, but never hives.

If I hadn't been properly trained in the Word, I could have easily spiraled downward into the world of food restrictions again. However, this time I fought back. I fought back with the truth of God's Word. I continued to eat the foods I desired and when I had a reaction I told that evil spirit that God had delivered me from the fear of food, and that it was a liar. I told it to stop tempting me, because I knew the truth. I'd been delivered of food sensitivities. I said this aloud and I also asked a friend to pray with me.

After about a week of resisting the devil, the hives stopped. Sometimes even though we've been delivered from an evil spirit, we can continue to have old thoughts, feelings and even physical manifestations. This is just temptation. God promises that if we submit ourselves to God and resist the devil, the devil will eventually flee from us (James 4:7).

Daily Maintenance

We can use the following acronym FREE to help maintain our deliverance and gain more ground from the enemy. God is faithful and He continues to give me fresh revelations. If I can do it, so can you!

> Step 2: Keep your house full & free
> **DAILY MAINTENANCE**: Health &protection, Mat 12:44
> **F**ight returning evil spirits (resist)
> **R**ead the Word
> **E**xpress your gratitude to God
> **E**quip other believers
>
> **Stay FREE!**

Remember we, can't do anything without God's power. Lean on Him. "Lord, keep me from falling" is my daily prayer! (Jude 24: "Now unto him that is able to keep you from falling, and to present you faultless before the presence of his glory with exceeding joy"").

Deliverance

I believe you've already begun noticing a difference in your life since you've started studying *Jesus Juice for Health and Freedom*. If not, keep studying your Bible and praising God and it will come. Lessons 1-6 led you in deliverance from unforgiveness, rejection, accusation, uncleanness, occultism and bondage, so you're probably feeling somewhat lighter and freer! Congratulations—"If the Son therefore shall make you free, ye shall be free indeed" (John 8:36). This is a good start. I bet you thought this was the end, lol.

Like other health regimens, Jesus Juice is a lifestyle change. The major difference is that Jesus Juice is founded on God's plan and He will help us day by day. Also, Jesus Juice is an absolutely free gift from God. It has NO SIDE EFFECTS and it is God approved.

God has given us power over evil spirits, but sometimes believers stay bound to unforgiveness, rejection, accusation, bondage, uncleanness and occultism because they don't know how to activate their God-given power (Hosea 4:6: "My people are destroyed for lack of knowledge: because thou hast rejected knowledge, I will also reject thee, that thou shalt be no priest to me: seeing thou hast forgotten the law of thy God, I will also forget thy children").

The Best Is Yet to Come!
Enjoy your new or renewed power over the enemy, but remember that being able to cast out evil spirits doesn't automatically qualify us for eternal salvation (Matthew 7:23: "Many will say to me in that day, Lord, Lord, have we not prophesied in thy name? and in thy name have cast out devils? and in thy name done many wonderful works? And then will I profess unto them, I never knew you: depart from me, ye that work iniquity"). Jesus clearly instructs us to "rejoice not, that the spirits are subject unto you; but rather rejoice, because your names are written in heaven" (Luke 10:20). Casting out evil spirits will give you a better life on earth, but nothing compares to the eternal life God promises believers in eternity.

I pray this book has been a blessing to you. To share your testimony or contact me for speaking engagements, visit www.jesusjuicebook.com or email tep@tp-rewards.com.

About the Author
Tenickia Ernestine Polk, Minister & Wellness Coach

Tenickia Polk is the founder of the TP Rewards Book Publishing Agency and the Victim Empowerment website, *DomesticViolence.tv*. Tenickia is also the host of the TV show *Community Chat*. Her passion for empowering people began with her own setbacks. Born into a disadvantaged community, she experienced violence and witnessed domestic abuse. Regrettably, Tenickia's struggles followed her throughout her early adult years, leading to homelessness, domestic abuse and a myriad of health issues. But with the encouragement of the gospel, mentors, programs and books, Tenickia was inspired to turn her life around.

Now Tenickia enjoys spreading education and inspiration through her TV show, books, seminars and the website *DomesticViolence.tv*. She serves as the Vice President of The Women's Group of Mt. Vernon, and is a marginalized/underserved population community representative to the Fairfax County Domestic Violence Prevention, Policy, and

Coordinating Council (DVPPCC). Tenickia shares her personal testimony of overcoming abuse and how she used biblical principles to overcome "incurable diseases" including lupus, chemical sensitivities, food sensitivities, and allergies, as well as mental blocks such as low self-esteem, fear, stress, anxiety, depression and more.

Lesson 1 Notes

Lesson 2 Notes

Lesson 3 Notes

Lesson 4 Notes

Lesson 5 Notes

Lesson 6 Notes

Lesson 7 Notes

Made in the USA
Charleston, SC
24 October 2015